Charisma

Increase Your Charisma and Ability to Influence People

(Improve Your Social Skills and Create Long Lasting Relationships With Everyone You Meet)

Stephen Mills

Published By **Chris David**

Stephen Mills

Charisma: Increase Your Charisma and Ability to Influence People (Improve Your Social Skills and Create Long Lasting Relationships With Everyone You Meet)

ISBN   978-1-7780570-5-2

Legal & Disclaimer

The information contained in this book is not designed to replace or take the place of any form of medicine or professional medical advice. The information in this book has been provided for educational & entertainment purposes only.

The information contained in this book has been compiled from sources deemed reliable, and it is accurate to the best of the Author's knowledge; however, the Author cannot guarantee its accuracy and validity and cannot be held liable for any errors or omissions. Changes are periodically made to this book. You must consult your doctor or get professional medical advice before using any of the suggested remedies, techniques, or information in this book.

Table Of Contents

Chapter 1: What Is Charisma?.................. 1

Chapter 2: Displays Confidence.............. 11

Chapter 3: Lack Of Independence 19

Chapter 4: Gain On Charisma................. 33

Chapter 5: How To Be Charismatic......... 46

Chapter 6: What Is Charisma?............... 63

Chapter 7: What Are The Characteristics Of A Charismatic Person? 81

Chapter 8: Understand The Different Types Of Charisma 86

Chapter 9: Why Should You Consider Developing Your Charisma? 92

Chapter 10: Exploring The Three Core Components Of Charisma 96

Chapter 11: What Do You Need To Have A Charismatic Attitude? 106

Chapter 12: Developing Your Confidence (Four Days).. 114

Chapter 13: Developing Your Social Skills (Four Days).. 129

Chapter 14: Developing Your Influence 143

Chapter 15: Developing Your Communication Skills............................ 165

Chapter 16: Developing Your Body Language 179

Chapter 1: What Is Charisma?

The basis of charisma dates all over again to the mid-1860s wherein it turn out to be first applied in taken into consideration certainly one of a kind Christian/non secular contexts. It is stated to consult a gift or determine upon, generally given to someone through using the Holy Spirit, (of which this revel in these days, may be very uncommon). In the non-spiritual context, the phrase 'air of secrecy' dates again to being first used within the yr 1922 in a German text published by way of the renowned Sociologist, Max Weber. And abruptly after Weber's artwork changed into published, the word started out to seem extra frequently in English publications.

It's standard expertise that we stay in a international made up of different human beings, from outstanding locations. The worldwide have become now not designed for its population to be an isolation of themselves. A man became created amongst others to learn how to cohabit. We need to understand that to relate as freely as we would really like with others, air of secrecy is needed. As I stated earlier, many human beings have idea air of secrecy to be a few factor that accompanies start, but it simply is not usually the case. Charisma can be determined out; it could be constructed, and it is advanced and labored upon. Charisma is truly the ability to endear, attraction, appeal to and draw the attention of people round you to yourself. Some different similarities of air of secrecy are equanimity, mystique, private enchantment and magnetism amongst many others.

The fact is many a time, human beings will forget about the utterances you could have made or the gestures you could have positioned up in regarding with them, but one element people will not often neglect approximately approximately you is, the manner you made them sense, especially in case you made them revel in all proper. Developing air of thriller for commercial enterprise enterprise agency and personal relationships may be very important, it can not be over emphasised. One of the clean, but very crucial dispositions of charisma improvement is 'enchantment.' Charm goes alongside air of thriller; they're nearly used interchangeably in a few contexts. Taking a examine billionaires, masses of people say "wonderful strokes for one-of-a-kind dad and mom," and as you recognize, it sincerely is real. Many of the billionaires we see in our society have specific strategies they placed as tons as pave their approaches into turning into billionaires, however one factor summarizes it for they all, that's 'Charisma,' so I'll name this the "Billionaire Way." The majority of them are charismatic. Naturally, human beings pant for a experience of friendship, belonging and acknowledgment. When you present yourself to humans in this form of way that it offers them a modified attitude about themselves, the reality is, they may be greater than willing to paintings with you and do matters for you. Once you get assist from people round you, it will likely be a large help, and your industrial organization will skyrocket. Charisma makes human beings in conjunction with you, makes human beings want to do subjects for you, and art work with you. Now, this should deliver no room for excuse to even the shyest man or woman on the planet. Just as I related in my story how I metamorphosed from being the shy little teen to the enchanter, the shy ones can determine to research from me. Charisma is decided terrific if you pick out to have a study.

Charisma - Good and Bad

I want you to recall this. While you have been more younger, you knew the manner to influence your dad and mom into imparting you with what you favored. Perhaps, you probably did no longer, you are pretty aware that hundreds of youngsters had the opportunity to. You may additionally need to influence them into searching for you a doll from one of the shops, or giving you the car because you had a date you did not need to overlook. Right? Great! That is because of the reality whilst you have been developing up, your parents were a bit a whole lot less tough to enchant than everyone else, no longer because you had been their little one, but due to the truth you made them experience appropriate approximately themselves. So, they were left and not using a preference than to offer you that that you preferred. The identical applies to the ones in enterprise organization, corporation societies, and the likes; the listing isn't always exhaustive. It's like a magnetic pressure. It will both attraction to or repel people inside the path of or an extended way from you. The way some humans are desired by means of others for no particular purpose is the equal way others aren't desired for any motive in besides. What makes the difference among those devices of people? It's their air of mystery; in fact placed, the way they painting/supply themselves, which brings us to the have a examine on specific or terrible charisma.

Good Charisma

Developing an tremendous air of mystery is probably very feasible. Once air of mystery has been determined, first rate communication and interpersonal abilities will not be tough for you. Appealing and incredible tendencies are continually connected to an high-quality air of mystery, and this plays out in the way you engage with splendid human beings, and on the flip element, repelling and awful dispositions are attached to terrible air of thriller. Good and awful charismas are used for both tremendous and terrible subjects. They produce each extraordinary or horrific quit end result. If you need to reveal proper charisma, then careful, deliberate and conscious hobby want to be paid to the manner you see yourself interacting with humans. A top charismatic individual makes use of his/her skills to advantage the attention of others. The hobby gotten from terrific humans is probably social, professional, or ideological. Outlined proper right here for you are a few strategies you can construct wonderful/real air of mystery.

Often, when you're asked to mention a charismatic character recognized to you, you're brief to mention politicians, celebrities or a few different public determine.

Of a truth, they are appeared as a hit because of their air of mystery, however there are also 'regular' individuals who own charismatic personalities. Unconventionally, it can be the very famous teen in university, the waiter/waitress who in an afternoon makes the maximum guidelines than others, that very well-known and great man or woman in the place of business or network, and plenty of others., the list is endless. Why will the ones human beings be regarded as a success? It is due to the air of mystery they painting. Check out your manner to being greater endearing under.

Shows Intelligence

As a good deal as a superb charismatic man or woman can speak efficiently, further they've got the functionality to start up conversations. A individual with proper aura continuously has an inclination to be knowledgeable and updated in almost everything. As stated inside the preamble of this discourse, the majority of the people who are said to be charismatic are the leaders, and because the well-known pronouncing goes "readers are leaders."

A man or woman with an notable air of mystery demonstrates intelligence. They inculcate in themselves, the functionality to examine. If you've got were given ever attended a project interview and left an surroundings of self notion after being interviewed, well, it's miles due to the truth you have have been given located out the artwork of being charismatic. A appropriate charismatic character commonly has expert expertise of wonderful regions, and they will interact others in a dialogue. When asked questions, they will be succesful to interrupt down the most complex trouble depend in a way that the aim marketplace completely is aware. The understanding as tested via using the usage of humans of precise air of mystery regularly motivates the self guarantee of others round them, similarly to others' beliefs in their talents.

Always Optimistic

Optimism; the capacity to always trust the pleasant out of a few component. Even even as confronted with the worst state of affairs, an optimist generally sees a manner out. A person with a wonderful charismatic individual generally suggests optimism. If you have ever noticed, humans are maximum interested in folks that offer solutions.

A character with an terrific aura is continuously glad and bubbly - now not regularly will you ever see them frown whilst in public. The capability to constantly be bubbly can encourage others. That way, others may be enthused and endorsed to be extra constructive but challenges, conditions or sports. If you have got in no manner been high fine, that is a danger that allows you to trade gears, and encourage other people round you.

Chapter 2: Displays Confidence

People who are charismatic are maximum times seemed as assured humans. Often, they are appeared as being proud with the aid of the ones who've did no longer see that they're most effective reflecting who they without a doubt are. The charismatic human beings typically pass a message to others round them that they very personal self notion. Over the years, you'll have seen instances of humans which have discovered it very difficult to talk correctly with others. The verbal exchange is probably one to 1, inside the front of an target marketplace, or perhaps in companies. You may additionally have even been a victim of this at one time or the alternative, as I became afore time. Charismatic human beings show self belief. They will in no manner consist of the concept of level fright although referred to as upon for a presentation. They are continuously prepared for impromptu sports at the manner to ought to do with dealing with a couple of person. And a top notch deal greater than showing self guarantee, someone with pinnacle aura additionally lets in others to revel in confident. It's like a perfume that is spread. Without displaying satisfaction or being immodest, desirable charismatic human beings communicate self perception honestly, as a give up result aiding the communication machine with others.

Causes Unity

For an superb/powerful verbal exchange to thrive, there needs to be concord. People with genuine air of mystery also have an assertive nature. They are usually boldly self-assured without being aggressive. Assertiveness makes you have got an effect at the people you relate with. Usually, the assertiveness of humans with first-rate air of thriller is mild, more like subtle. They are able to persuade the humans they relate with, with their words, with out manipulations, inspire them via their effective nature and the self guarantee they personal.

Pays Attention to Details

To be someone with proper air of mystery consists of paying near interest to statistics. You have to be meticulous sufficient. During dynamic communication, enthusiasm and amazing frame language must be communicated. Paying interest to information is part of what makes an excellent aura, and the element of the how of interpersonal courting. Empathize with others whilst important, and show sympathy in which it's desired. It offers a enjoy of belonging to whomever you're relating to with.

Good at Playing with Emotions

Although at certain times, whilst matters art work to the benefit of pinnacle charismatic human beings, they are top at displaying their emotions. But on the same time, a person with exceptional air of mystery is likewise able to persuade others to see matters the manner he needs them to see it. It is synonymous to the swimming swan. On the ground of the water is the very smooth-going, seemingly terrific swan, however underneath the water is a whole lot of struggles and combat, within the bid to keep transferring. A correct charismatic man or woman is likewise an sensible, emotional participant. They are normally incredible at concealing proper feelings and making humans accept as genuine with what they see from them. If you want to reveal effective tendencies of an brilliant air of thriller, then you may furthermore look at the art of making humans bear in mind what they see from you.

Shows Interest in People and are Interesting themselves

One of the very exciting subjects approximately humans with actual air of secrecy is that they may be exciting beings. No one likes to normally be round uninteresting human beings. Being thrilling attracts people the more to you. A particular charismatic persona is an interesting one-people usually want to take note of them. They also are concerned - they typically like to take note of people. It's balanced; one would no longer go through on the cost of the opportunity. Often, they will be storytellers, proper ones at that, with the ability to engage the minds of the humans taking note of them. When speaking, they'll be concise and clean, excessive and at the equal time humorous. They realize while to infuse humor into their talks inside the bid to hold their goal marketplace focused.

They apprehend the precise kinesis to apply at the same time as appealing people, each in small institution discussions, one on one talks, or a presentation to a huge target audience. When on one-on-one discussions, they will be attempting to maintain eye touch, the usage of body languages. They additionally constantly try to get feedbacks from their audience to make clean what has been said to them. On the alternative hand, while in a larger agency, they exaggerate their body language a piece extra to cope with anyone.

You can display interest in others with the aid of the usage of generally asking questions to understand the perspectives of others, and in move lower back, because of your capability to make others relaxed, and calm anxiety, you'll get honest solutions, as human beings can be with out problem spread out to you. You don't need to attend to be excellent of friends with the people you relate with, the only critical aspect needed is to steer them that you're interested by them, and the most correct way is thru without a doubt being interested by them.

Bad Charisma

Just as we recognize the alternative of proper to be awful, it honestly is the equal way the opportunity of real air of secrecy is likewise terrible air of mystery. If you don't have an fantastic aura or have not perception it match to boom an terrific air of thriller, then you can be stated to have a lousy air of secrecy. When a exceptional charismatic character endear humans to themselves, the alternative is the case of terrible charismatic people. As extended as air of mystery remains a gift, it endears humans to you, however the negative element approximately awful air of thriller is that human beings take gain of the truth that they have aura, and use it to take benefit of others. Care for the excellent information? It can be labored on. What will honestly be required of you will be to take a look at yourself thru the factors that'll be listed. If at one point or the alternative, you have fallen a sufferer, or presently are a victim, it's far never past due to expose matters around. Bad air of mystery can be modified for the better. We all want specific effects. It's like Garbage In, Garbage Out - what you put in is what you may get out. If you sow seeds of self notion in humans, you get self guarantee from them. Actually, if you take a eager observe aura, you'd realize that air of thriller in itself isn't a terrible factor. Remember, its meaning is 'present', and items recommend goodness. As a recall of reality, it should continuously produce remarkable outcomes but what if a villain takes region to have aura? Let's take a look at some key topics about people who show terrible aura.

Chapter 3: Lack Of Independence

When humans come collectively to artwork as a set, and a charismatic character occurs to be in that agency, on occasion, it makes the opposite business enterprise people shift reputation and vicinity it at the only who has aura. And the reality is, at the equal time as humans in a group have delegated the artwork to you because of the fact you've got what it takes to keep on, you could comprehend. Rather than calling the eye of others, and inspiring them to anticipate on their very personal to get consequences, you revel in precise about your self, and determine to take the complete obligation on yourself. This type of thoughts-set will now not assist others to build self-fortitude and act independently at the identical time as on their personal.

Under-Acknowledgment of the Strength of Others

Most particularly even as a charismatic character is in rate of an enterprise, the humans jogging underneath him may additionally in some unspecified time in the destiny start to assume that the fulfillment of the commercial enterprise business enterprise is tied to the leader, finally, needless acknowledgments. They overlook the success is because of the joint strive with the useful resource of method of every member of the enterprise. And by way of a few approach, it starts offevolved to get to the top of the charismatic man or woman that he begins offevolved to enjoy in truth tremendous about himself, no longer minding others.

Tightened Countenance

Just like I stated, you do no longer need to be exquisite of pals with a person before you get that roller coaster acquaintance dating going. There genuinely is not any damage in being the most effective to increase the hand of friendship. When you do not flow the greater mile to expose interest within the humans round you, you can never be seen as charismatic. If you're constantly sporting a tightened countenance, it's time to lighten up and get extra human beings inquisitive about you. A get dressed with out a smile, they are saying, is incomplete, and terrible aura includes not setting up a smile.

Overtaken with the aid of the usage of Pride

Sometimes, charismatic people get over ridden by way of their ego after they get too caught up by way of using what they've been able to gain. Bad air of mystery propels you to be too whole of yourself like nobody matters. At one-of-a-type times, awful air of thriller makes you experience above the regulation, in the end violating moral suggestions and codes of conduct, that is usually pushed via way of ego. Pride, due to lousy air of thriller will make you now not need to analyze from your errors, ultimately making you unresponsive to corrections from others around you.

Achievable with Charisma

Have you ever carried out a few aspect, and felt so pretty of your self? You apprehend the manner it feels whilst you've had a first-rate accomplishment of a specific aspect. Whenever you take a planned motion within the route of something/anything, you are maximum truely looking beforehand to to get effects/see answers. That's the manner it works with air of secrecy. Over time, while human beings look at the art of charming others with air of mystery, they begin to see consequences absolutely specific from the ones they may were getting afore time. Just as a expert chippie will make an excellent looking chair out of simply wooden, he needed to take planned movements to get that chair. If you want to get consequences like I have come to be able to within the course of middle university, you need to art work on your air of mystery. Charisma brings results, and beneath are a number of the consequences produced. Enjoy and determine to get higher, because of the truth as a consider quantity of fact, you could get higher.

1. Sell Visions

As mentioned in this discourse, I changed into capable of lay the muse that charismatic people are such that display hobby in people, by using using being interesting themselves. If you have got were given a vision and function now not the charisma for it, your vision will only live as a mirage to you. Most of the time, charismatic human beings get people to ride together with them, even as they'll be way beyond suitable at selling their vision. By selling a vision, how do I suggest? I genuinely suggest the capability to outline the form of destiny you observe and need to create. In precise terms, it is the capability to permit human beings purpose what may be about a few component. Through the charming personalities of charismatic people, they are constantly capable of make humans see the larger image, and purchase into the huge dream. For the charismatic man, nothing is unachievable. As lengthy as you could dream it, you may moreover have it.

2. Interpersonal friendliness

The wellknown positive and first-class person of a charismatic character draws human beings to themselves. It evokes friendliness amongst others and motivates others to be the high-quality at a few factor they is probably doing. It cuts at some point of the walking surroundings; charismatic people preserve a immoderate level of friendliness amongst humans alike.

three. Get effects

Often, people cross all out to get subjects accomplished for the captivating persona. Not due to the fact they'll be charming in themselves, but due to the truth they had been able to instill self assurance within the people they relate with efficaciously. Want to constantly get consequences? Then attempt to be a hint more charismatic. You'll discover that humans may be willing to get topics finished in your benefit. Charismatic human beings never lose.

four. Gives you what you need

People who are charismatic are normally sturdy willed. They get what they need, even at the identical time as no longer having to work an excessive amount of for it. Once a charismatic individual has set his eyes on the ball, he stops at no longer some thing until the ball has been performed into the net (figuratively). For example, someone who attends a manner interview, and shows amazing air of thriller can be desired above others who didn't show charisma. Good air of mystery sends a message to people which you're capable of what you need, as a result, developing an factor for you over and above others.

5. Effects changes

A charismatic person can effect changes - exquisite changes, it really is normally because of their heightened zeal, enthusiasm, and electricity. Not only leaders are charismatic. As I earlier stated, even 'normal' human beings are. Team leaders are typically triggered with the aid of way of using the keenness and enthusiasm of people with air of mystery to obtain extra while there may be cause to paintings together. They are extra frequently regarded to the using stress in any placing they discover themselves.

Missing Charisma

Ever been in a spot in which you felt you were eligible to get a few factor, however in a few way left out out on that aspect? Well, the maximum oldsters have. When your thoughts has been settled on getting/accomplishing some thing, and also you don't in the end get it, the edge it motives. Missing air of thriller creates a barrier amongst you and your aim, and the only manner to help yourself at the equal time as effects aren't coming forth is to have a take a look at yourself and note in which you lack charisma. Lack of charisma deprives you of loads of factors, and a few might be tested on this discourse.

What you pass over if your man or woman lacks charisma:

I'd say an entire lot. Once air of secrecy is from your man or woman, an entire lot is out. Character and air of secrecy are like a chain tied to the other. However, to say but a few may be, for the case of this have a study.

You miss out on friends. Friends are made to make life much less complex for us. When you lack air of secrecy, in some way, you become an isolation of your self.

You might not be able to prove a point, even whilst you understand outrightly what you are trying to reveal. You might also moreover moreover notable be able to in case you come upon the definitely pleasant human beings.

If you don't very own air of secrecy as a part of your character, you could end up missing out on possibilities.

Bad Situations

On some days, awful topics appear. On distinct days, actually lousy topics seem. Life may also additionally furthermore decide to get complex on you, leaving you with simply options: half self-piety and condemned, or select out positivity and create some thing awesome out of the apparently lousy state of affairs. Having pals to undergo life with us is a vital necessity. Human relationships are almost as crucial because the necessities of meals, secure haven, and garb. Not anybody in your lifestyles has come to live; whilst some come as a lesson, others come as a blessing. When buddies are modified, and charisma is missing, it will become difficult to get acquainted with the modern-day set of humans coming your way. At incredible instances, it is able to be relocation because of a catastrophe or a few aspect; in case your person lacks air of secrecy, consider me after I say getting to relate together in conjunction with your new set of friends will appear like an impossibility to you. A few illustrations to buttress horrible situations. You are standing right in the front of a big target market who're searching ahead to your presentation, looking for you to expose them your ultra-modern initiative. Your palms are all sweaty.

The phrases are not even coming forth from your mouth. Or you occur to be appointed due to the fact the employees as a way to confront a totally amazing, but underperforming co-employee at artwork, and produce him back on course? How will you be able to placed up with those varieties of if the air of secrecy is missing? At one factor or the opposite, we had been in almost as tight conditions like this. What takes location subsequent? There is certainly not something on the way to are available in on hand at this juncture than bringing out the air of thriller in to play. Once you're able to offer you with a fascinating and motivating a message that captivates the minds of your target marketplace, you're pinnacle to move, and this could quality come about thru air of mystery; the greater reason air of mystery desires to be observed and intentionally worked upon.

On the alternative hand, what takes area to a person who's unfair, and has air of mystery? If a person takes area to be a charismatic character and is treacherous, this type of one will take advantage of others. Charisma is meant to be a present and used appropriately to derive wonderful consequences, and no longer the alternative way spherical. When your person is missing air of mystery, right intentions now and again may be seen as terrible. For example, mimics, body languages, voice, eye contacts and the likes. The fundamental concept inside the lower returned of retaining eye contact whilst having a communication with someone is to maintain the verbal exchange flowing, and recognize that you every have each great in the way. However, even as someone who hasn't mastered the attraction in air of thriller and maintaining eye contact does it, they may keep eye touch to such an volume that the alternative individual starts offevolved to recognize insubordination. Maintaining eye contact in itself is in no manner awful, but whilst not used efficaciously sends the wrong message, and it's identical with body language and voice. Usually, humans are sending loads of alerts with body posture and language, and those messages usually have extended-lasting repercussions. Choose accurately- ought to you want to be remembered for proper or terrible after having interacted with a person? While many elements of frame language and nonverbal communication exist, one component that can assist us popularity greater on people's comfort or soreness is getting to know to look how they experience, anticipate, fear or maybe what they preference. When you have got that extra perception, you'll be given a extra sincere appraisal with the useful resource of the usage of others, thereby, fostering extra effective verbal exchange. But what in case you're no longer able to appearance things from the mind-set of others? Keep it at coronary heart that charismatic human beings display empathy whilst crucial. When you lack air of mystery, there may be no manner verbal exchange may be powerful, and it deprives you of possibilities on some sports. If you are not able to steer a capacity business agency (inside the organization worldwide) that you have what it takes to get you on that machine, there may be in no manner a way you are getting the method. Someone as a substitute who suggests air of mystery, and dispels a revel in of firmness and self belief to capability employers will without issue get a task if interviewed at the identical platform with every other with out aura.

Chapter 4: Gain On Charisma

Although there may also moreover were debates approximately aura being both innate or discovered, the two views aren't together terrific of themselves. While a few are of the opinion that humans are born with air of mystery, others are of the opinion that it is observed. My view on this? Well, I will not categorically u . S . A . That humans are born charismatic or humans learn to have air of secrecy due to the reality as a matter amount of fact, a few are born charismatic. By this, I propose they have got the tendency to express air of thriller at the equal time as grown up, on the equal time as some are born timid. If you have ever observed youngsters and the way they have interaction with themselves while playing, I bet you may almost constantly tell who the charismatic ones are, and who the shy ones are. Having aura as an innate capability by myself cannot maintain you. When it is been determined as a trait, the outstanding you may do for yourself is to paintings on it to be better at what you do, and on how human beings understand you. Charisma may be found out. If you are part of those who've in no way visible a trait of being charismatic, it isn't always too past because of study the artwork of commanding the attention of others. I had this as a extremely good difficulty at the same time as developing up, and although it wasn't a humorous revel in, I changed into capable of scale via and ruin forth, and now, I can boldly permit you to apprehend that it takes high-quality consistency in exercise to see what you in fact want to look. Nothing is unachievable; if you could dream it, you could stay it.

Charisma is not all innate. It's additionally learnable. If you supply yourself to extra exercise, you would see yourself being greater attractive, influential and agree with worthy. It's like setting a infant in college. You located him/her in school to learn how to observe and write. After masses schooling, the child is capable of positioned letters together and pronounce them as phrases. It's a machine. Although the manner of studying air of thriller won't be as grievous as a infant passing through college to analyze. However, it is well worth of word that there are some topics that you'll want to artwork on to look your self dispensing that appeal to others, and I will like to call this 'self-improvement.'

How to Improve on Yourself

and Shine on Others

On many activities, when you flow into route with new people, you really need to create an superb, prolonged-lasting impact that permits you to cause them to want to nonetheless meet with you at later times; you genuinely need to be as likable as possible. If this has proved surely abortive in the past for you, and also you discover it difficult trying to turn the enchantment on, then there may be some subjects which you haven't labored on, on your self, growing the bridge among you and the human beings you meet. You can't manage humans into liking you or searching for to get close to, you may terrific attempt with the beneficial aid of being captivating, and that demeanor of enchantment comes best from air of thriller- from internal to outside. There are some guidelines with a view to go through and paintings on, for this reason improving yourself and getting the shine to rub off on specific. Enjoy!

Learn to concentrate more: it is more honorable to pay attention to others than being the only talking. If simplest all and sundry understood this, I assume the arena may additionally want to have a super range of listeners with the useful aid of now, and as we apprehend, listeners are most instances solution providers. In the artwork of listening, you don't constantly need to respond verbally. Engage non-verbal communication as well. People love people that take time to be aware about what they've to mention. Release beams of smile at durations; nod your head while small talks are on. Most instances, that is nearly all it takes for the other person to revel in important. When you are given the possibility to talk or deem it wholesome to reduce in, I'd advise you do no longer be in haste to provide advice. Listening in itself sends a message to the opposite individual which you care, now not that you're in haste to provide advice, due to the fact in nearly commonly, at the same time as it is all about advice in a verbal exchange, then it sends a message that the communication changed into about you, and now not the alternative character.

Render the prevailing of your complete time.

Don't make the possibility person feel like a criminal obligation. Try to area your stuff away at the same time as you have engaged yourself with any other person. The reality is, you may hardly connect with others whilst a part of you is mounted to important stuff which encompass your cell cellphone. Do the opportunity character the honour of placing away your cell smartphone inside the suggest time, at the least.

Gently select out the phrases you operate.

Be diplomatic inside the use of your phrases to others. People are often endeared to those who have gained mastery in the right use of terms, and show of thoughts-set. For instance, you could now not always say "you are going for a meeting." You can also need to without issues say "I'm going to sign up for a few exceptional cool humans and rub thoughts with them." You do not have to mention you may the gymnasium; you could say "you are going for walks out to maintain fit and healthful."

You don't always need to benefit achievement to be charismatic. As everyday as you are, be humble. Accept your failings specifically regions, and take a look at classes from your mistakes. Don't be on the lookout for the mistakes of others. Watch out for yours moreover, admit and examine from them.

Improve on scanning the body language

You have to additionally enhance on scanning the frame language of others. Nothing appears to be appealing in interrupting solitary moments through someone who desires to be left on my own at a selected second. The reality that someone wants to be left by myself in a few unspecified time within the future does now not imply at other elements; such fellow would not be interested in interacting. Know even as to consist of yourself inside the communication of others; whilst you do, you end up more likable, and that they get to understand the truth which you apprehend their alternatives. That's encouraging in case you inquire from me.

Approach humans with a grin; a confident smile.

Get used to smiling constantly. A smile is ready the precise enchantment each person can positioned on; it sends loads of messages to others. Have you idea approximately this-how could you furthermore mght want a person to technique you, and what is going to be your response while a person probable techniques you with a frown? A smile makes humans more cushty and sends a message which you're not a threat to them. It also makes them feel like you are in fact having a fantastic time with your self, in the long run, developing an environment for them to be extra comfortable with you. It is, however, genuinely really worth to phrase that the wrong kind of smile is manner better than now not even giving a smile inside the first example. Always hold your smile real.

Relationships Gain on Charisma

As a necessity of life and a experience of belonging, relationships are vital; be it circle of relatives, romantic, organization, or industrial organization relationships; at one factor or the opposite, better even though, at every factor, we need relationships. I want relationship, you furthermore mght need. No one is excluded on this chain. Relationships decorate while there may be a excellent display of air of secrecy. In own family relationships, we are nearly constantly very pleased with that brother or sister of ours it is very well-known in faculty, like yeah, it sincerely is my brother. You'll constantly want to be identified with that specific sibling, this is quite normal. A heightened feel of belonging is in reality created on the equal time as a member in a cycle has air of thriller. Talk approximately romantic relationships- for guys which can be very assured, you will phrase that their women are normally very consistent at the same time as round them, expertise that their men will continuously find out a way to supply them out of any scenario they will discover themselves in, at any element in time. In industrial agency relationships, charisma permits you close to making income. If you do not show aura in commercial enterprise enterprise, you would in all likelihood in no way be convincing sufficient to capability customers. And as studied, charismatic people are sensible, emotional players- they may be capable of making you recollect what you note; this trait is drastically important in commercial enterprise corporation. To gain success in all rounds of human relationships, take a look at air of thriller. The funding in mastering charisma can pay massive dividends in your relationships.

Kinds of Charisma

As has been stated nearly during this discourse, one of the very most vital talents all of us want to increase is air of secrecy. It's not exhaustive for each person. Just the manner the sky is big enough for every chook t fly, air of mystery can not be said to be for a specific set of people. Anyone and all of us can be charismatic. When used efficiently, it's powerful and is a determinant to 3 easy matters for you inclusive of getting a task, being promoted at your workplace or being able to make a particular sale as a sales man or woman. However, for the sake of this have a look at, we'll be searching at the sorts of air of mystery from 4 (4) views viz:

1. Visionary

2. Focus

three. Authority

4. Kindness

Visionary Charisma

Vision is one mission that might in no way be over emphasized whilst discussing air of thriller. To show visionary air of mystery, you want to be proactive, personal a future template, efficaciously communicate your imaginative and prescient to others and encourage them to key into the large photograph. One worry that has typically been of man is that of the unknown; uncertainty. Once humans had been able to see that you in reality do have a plan, they'll be inclined to recognize to you.

Focus Charisma

The critical component of cognizance is 'recognize and understanding of emotions.' Many oldsters have that unique pal we're able to open up to approximately any/everything- our concerns, goals, fears and the likes. They're continuously with out troubles to be had to us. Focus air of mystery makes human beings understand which you recognize how they enjoy. In this form of air of mystery, eye contact can be very critical. Through it, and occasional nodding of your head, you are able to skip a message to them which you're listening on the equal time as placing phrases as "I apprehend" or "sure" to reveal which you're associated.

Authority Charisma

One factor I'd which includes you to reckon with is the truth that, the area's best leaders recorded in statistics are folks that were capable of command authority. You don't have to wait to be a leader to command apprehend and authority. In authority air of thriller, body language is pinnacle. You need to discover ways to take control of your moves- purpose them to comfortable and a bit sluggish. When you're cool and calm, you undertaking a standing of self perception and authority to the ones spherical you.

Kindness Charisma

Some human beings are simply whole of high quality vibes and capable of spreading love everywhere they locate themselves. Have you ever come upon such human beings? They own kindness air of thriller. It's essentially about having a magnetic attraction to create an environment of warmth and making others sense welcome without any iota of inferiority complicated. In the development of this aura, body language is likewise important. You'll strive as hundreds as viable to keep away from terrible frame gestures with the useful resource of first taking a test the opportunity character's frame language, consequently, developing receive as true with and allowing them to be sincere with you.

Chapter 5: How To Be Charismatic

I choose out out to apply this concern rely because of the truth now not anybody has determined out to be charismatic, and I want it to be that, on the cease of this discourse, you'd be challenged in addition to brought about to create that appeal you in no manner have created, and draw extra people to you. You need to also word that amidst the heightened feelings of looking to be charismatic, it comes with responsibilities. It isn't supposed to be a name to laziness.

Ever pondered on how a few humans can almost seize the attention of definitely anybody? By absolutely really all and sundry, I mean anybody! It does now not rely the popularity of that individual, as quickly as such someone strategies anywhere, the complete hobby is regular on that man or woman, and even as this sort of one exits a premise, human beings might glaringly just need to be like them?

Body Language and Posture

Posture is basically characterized as body language. Charismatic humans are normally very business enterprise in their posture. I don't assume whatever photographs real self perception the manner posture does. Showing appropriate posture may be very vital as long as aura is involved. If you take a near test charismatic people stand, they stand tall, and when they stroll, they stroll everyday, now not sheepishly. When you input a room complete of unusual faces, stroll in with satisfaction, and live up for embracing new possibilities. When you stand, stand right now, while you sit, furthermore make certain to sit at once, not bent. When you convert pleasantries with a trendy character for the first time, offer a enterprise, but friendly handshake. Let the whole lot approximately your frame language be displayed as pleasant. When engaged in a communicate with someone, make sure to sit down coping with the character, and try as an entire lot as possible in your fingers to be saved far from your face. To show charisma to your walking posture, it have to be ensured which you don't stroll together with your head bent. Charisma speaks honestly the language of self belief, and self perception involves you walk together together with your head up; it sends a message of "yo worldwide, I'm out on your taking in recent times." Often instances, humans are cheated while their countenances specific timidity, it's frequently displayed thru looking all of the manner down to the floor. Keep your head up, in conjunction with your shoulders right now. There's not some factor appealing about having shrugged shoulders at the same time as on foot.

There are a few topics I'd like to usher in your word approximately posture. Remember posture is prepared your carriage even as walking, fame, and sitting or being in any characteristic. However, for the sake of this have a observe, I'll speak essentially on fame and sitting. Here are some forbidden belongings you ought to recognize about posture that can help you in being greater charismatic.

While on seat, as plenty as viable, keep away from slouching in your chair. It is beneficial you take a seat down straight away to enhance beneficial resource out of your muscle groups. Straight sitting dependancy emanates air of mystery.

Posing a posture of hunched again even as sitting isn't always a number of a fantastic idea. As lots as feasible, your neck ought to be lengthened upwards with a tucked in chin.

When for your feet, keep away from pushing your backside out. Ensure your shoulders are snug, with your belly pulled in on the equal time as your knees are also cushty, and your legs right now.

Avoid placing pressure on one leg on the equal time as reputation, with the alternative snug. It acquired't speak properly of you if you want to reveal aura.

While on a smartphone, keep away from placing your cellphone in amongst your ears and shoulder. As a good buy as feasible, preserve your smartphone efficiently in conjunction with your hand.

The Mirror Practice

Try the mirror exercising. I keep in mind doing mimics of my dad while developing up. I'd stand right in the front of the replicate in his room and talk to myself as even though he had been the exceptional speaking to me. And the humorous problem changed into, I'd reply as me. Funny, isn't it? But it helped me grasp the paintings of my dad's talking. I even have turn out to be used to it proper away. I recommend you get a status replicate and exercise right inside the the front of it. Act a presentation and watch yourself. In the approach, I'd want you to take a close to check your frame actions, gestures, and posture. Look at your eyes- what do they recommend? Your arms - do they endorse you as being charismatic or truly a few exclusive timid man or woman? Are you capable of experience from your imaginary congregation that someone feels the emotion you're trying to find to skip in the course of? The replicate exercise may be of excellent assist at the same time as you continue to be normal with it, revealing the components that want to be worked on.

It may be essential you have a observe, then imitate the body language of the human beings you are engaged in a communication with. This way, you'll be capable of get nearer, no longer in a verbal manner, but non-verbal. When you observe that someone makes use of gestures lots, you need to make your self nearer via the usage of gestures moreover, and when a person wants to be left on my own, do nicely now not to make wild gestures.

Eye Contact Maintenance

Develop the addiction of preserving eye touch. No one wants to be in a conversation with a person who appears to be over excited. Try to look human beings in the attention whilst having a dialogue. In the manner of maintaining eye contact, you don't must look on this sort of way that stares the opposite man or woman down. At some factor, you may go searching the room, not to signify you as being shy, but to guide them to enjoy you're not trying to oppress them collectively at the side of your appearance. Know that you don't simplest engage humans collectively together with your voice. You also can use your eyes to engage people in a communication.

Give a actual smile, not a faux one. Your smile will say a whole lot even earlier than starting your mouth to mention a few issue. It will permit the people you're approximately to engage with understand which you absolutely are interested by them. Give compliments freely and as a whole lot as possible, permit your compliments constantly be real, and on the equal time, embody comments freely from human beings when they provide it to you.

Sense of Humor

To be charismatic, you have to be capable of make human beings chortle. It's the appeal of being witty. When you can make others laugh very without difficulty without tough trials, then you definately definately've won their hearts. People don't generally enjoy silly interactions. Engage others with a excellent chortle. Sometimes, clearly giggle at yourself. Once you've discovered out the way to snort at, and to your self, human beings may be interested by you. It will tell them how loads self notion you've got were given in yourself. In guffawing at your self, try not to be self-depreciating. When you are, you are making your flaws very apparent to others, and in place of laughing with you, humans will giggle at you. Therefore, there must be a stability.

Don't be too uptight that you forget about others, and don't comic story round. People appeared to be charismatic are normally in sync with the funny capacity of these round them. In one-of-a-type phrases, they already apprehend the humorousness of the people engaged in communicate with them. Note that the caliber of human beings you communicate with is a determinant of the form of jokes you drop. When engaged with humans which may be truely offensive of their humor, I anticipate you don't be afraid to play alongside. On the other hand, while engaged with aged parents, or you are in a more touchy surroundings, your humor ought to be toned down, and attempt as plenty as feasible to keep your jokes brief and masses much less offensive. Charisma teaches you to play together with what exists. You truly do no longer need to see your self turning others off along aspect your jokes misused. Note that jokes aren't in themselves horrible, however they emerge as lousy while used in irrelevant contexts.

Don't almost put on yourself out inside the bid to be humorous. Jokes do now not want to be cracked every 5 to 10 seconds to reveal which you've got the wits. Place more emphasis on excellent than amount, due to the truth in the end, it's miles the nice if you want to always win. Just the excellent shaggy dog tale that is properly-timed can pass an extended way after a conversation.

Learn the paintings of teasing human beings. When you've got determined each person to be comfortable round you, strive joking round by means of teases. Your teases need to be less offensive regardless of the fact that. When you with out issues tease, it could endear the individual more to you, and deliver the individual the perception that while crucial as you could every now and then be, you do no longer take the entirety too severe.

Enthusiasm

Show enthusiasm, zeal, willingness, availability, ardour, and electricity. Give the belief that you're typically inclined to be of help in which need be. It's a pleasant mind-set of charismatic people, and the more you display yourself to be available, the greater human beings can even reply to be available to you. Give high-quality vibes as I'll say. Enthusiasm also can be expressed to your writing, talking, listening and speakme talents. How you're able to effortlessly unique your self will to a massive amount, show your air of mystery degree. Have you top notch ardour for writing? Why now not attempt locating out a few YouTube motion pics that beautify extremely good writing talents?

Knowledge they may be announcing is in no manner an excessive amount of. Increase your air of thriller via getting extra information from experts in fields as public speaking, writing or listening. You may additionally determine to transport the extra mile with the useful resource of arranging on line meetings genuinely in the bid to connect with the ones professionals and benefit more know-how on being charismatic. Take up on-line charismatic courses and be extra expert in its software program in your every day way of life. There are sorts of charisma development videos them on the net which you could download and watch at your comfort. It's now not a awful idea you move for such.

In all, allow enthusiasm be your drive, for in case you in no manner display ardour for a specific component, you may never advantage mastery in it.

Dressing

On dressing and display of self belief, go through in thoughts that in case you want to seem assured, you need to appearance confident. You cannot placed on a assured look and display timidity. It might not work that manner. A well-known saying is going therefore "the manner you get dressed is how you may be addressed," and I be part of that. Even whilst however walking on internal self guarantee, an outward appearance of self belief will portray you as being confident, of which dressing is a part. Expensive clothes do now not decide air of mystery. You should also be on cheap garments, however with a confident appearance, people may be forced to look far out of your clothes, and emulate your character. On the opportunity hand, if you may come up with the cash for expensive clothing, thoroughly then. They deliver out the self assure in you, even whilst you do no longer have it. The concept of relevant/charismatic garb isn't all approximately being neatly dressed on my own, for there are people who dress properly and display no air of thriller. On the manner to being charismatic with dressing, I receive as authentic with the ones few pointers can help out.

Take case studies of charismatic people on-line, and research from their get dressed revel in. I trust a whole lot of us enroll in followership on social media handles as Facebook, Instagram, Twitter and the likes. How about searching how they move approximately their garments and combinations? Just the manner greatness isn't effects accomplished, as there are continuously prices to pay, to come to be as charismatic in dressing because the humans you appearance as plenty as on social media, be prepared to pay the fee. Subscribing to their YouTube channels may be costly, however it's suitable I remind you that correct matters don't come clean. If your intended 'net mentor' is the shoe type and also you're the sandals kind, it's now not a horrible concept you circulate the greater mile to get a few shoes and be exactly like that person you look as tons as.

Learn to in shape colorings successfully. There's not anything as attractive as being with a bit of success dressed and out. It boosts your self confidence and esteem. If I maintain in mind successfully, I actually have become taught another time then in considered one in every of our Fine Arts commands the way it's appalling to mix primary hues. It's quality to mention that technology has taken over the world, and getting even the most complicated of things accomplished effects isn't a ways-fetched all over again. Get on google, surf on outstanding fabric coloration mixtures, and attempt them out likewise. It drops on you an air of secrecy of aura which you won't be capable of help however spread to others.

Wearing tremendous colognes construct aura. You may additionally have forgotten to combine shades efficiently, however the perfume of your cologne is probably sufficient to cowl up the oversight of awful coloration aggregate. Nice body sprays collect self warranty, which in flip builds air of thriller.

Absolutely nothing terrible in being your fashion inventor. A popular saying is going consequently "in each nonsense, there's a experience." Which approach that you may determine to increase your very personal fashion, which could without trouble be completed through going through sorts of patterns at the internet, and rejigging thru them to fit your self.

Talents and Hobbies

Hobbies are sports you like to partake in for the sake of rest or satisfaction. Take some time to loosen up alongside pals on the same time as gambling your hobby. It is probably a avenue stroll, baseball, basketball, football or any form of game you enjoy doing. Make them see how a exquisite deal mastery you have were given acquired inside the ones fields, and engage them in talks approximately them. Sooner than later, you will see others registering hobby to your hobby, and you, getting the more likable via them. When human beings start to reveal interest in your interest, they see you as being exciting to them. If you're gifted with a selected understanding, have a few element to reveal for it. Dance in which critical if you're precise at it. Sometimes, you may even need to head a piece loopy. Who cares? Get concerned in companies and activities which may be analogous for your competencies. When human beings see you for who you're, they get interested in you, and will virtually need to recognize you extra.

Self-Respect

Treat your self with love and understand. Take a while to spoil yourself. As a girl, you do now not normally need to appearance in advance to a man to take you out; and as a man, you do now not always always need to be within the commercial enterprise business enterprise of a girl earlier than you bypass on a treat. Show a few recognize for yourself. If you have got the manner, invite friends over, no damage in being the only to take them out for a drink or meal. In essence, simply be yourself, be genuine, be original, and permit others admire you for who you are.

Chapter 6: What Is Charisma?

What is Charisma, and How to be Charismatic?

In the Greek language, air of thriller is derived from 'Kharisma,' translated as "grace given" or "freely given want." This captivating beauty and attraction have the potential to encourage purity and devotion in people who are exposed to it. It is once in a while called "conferred talents" or "conferred electricity." According to three, air of secrecy is an exquisite combination of interpersonal abilities and exquisite communique talents. These capabilities can be decided and devolved, making it feasible to have a strong presence of charisma. When combined, the ones modern-day and complex social and emotional talents have the capacity to convert an person from invisible to invincible in an right now. Charismatic human beings might also have an effect on and feature an effect on others on an emotional degree. They do that with the aid of the use of developing sturdy interpersonal connections and speaking correctly.

Charisma is regularly belief of as a character trait, but it in reality refers to the capability to steer others. While air of mystery has many special components, some key components embody connecting with humans in detail, being persuasive, and having a brilliant presence. While it's miles often associated with leaders and public figures, air of thriller may be decided in all forms of people.

That one-of-a-kind and excellent know-how make you stand out even whilst you aren't trying very difficult. It isn't always essential to be obnoxious and stentorian to attain fulfillment. However, that magnetic air of mystery captures absolutely everyone's interest and piques their interest to such an quantity. It should now not be pressured with bodily elegance or any superpower, however as an alternative with a private magnetism that may purpose you to be cherished, preferred, and praiseworthy in the eyes of people who've a examine you.

But how are you going to broaden this type of magnetic personality, you'll likely surprise? Well...

The first step inside the path of growing air of secrecy is to boom one's self-self assure and self-esteem. Be self-confident without discovering as conceited or immodest. Others will feel the same way about you if you are powerful and confident for your very very very own capabilities. Self-assure will help you expand an irresistible charisma an extremely good way to draw others' hobby. Acquire mastery and information in any vicinity of hobby to you because it's miles the muse of self-self notion. Possessing capabilities and sources allows you to delve into the maximum in-intensity of topics, and it has a profound impact on the way you convey yourself and experience approximately yourself. A assured character allows to enhance communique with the aid of using developing a excessive incredible consolation place and removing any obstacles that may be gift during the exchange of terms.

One trait that all charismatic people percentage is their capability to stay positive inside the face of adversity. Although air of thriller and self belief aren't synonymous, exuding self perception need to make you appear greater charismatic. For trouble-solving and a hit negotiation, optimism and amazing questioning can be extremely effective and dependable forces to attract on. Maintaining a cheerful and bubbly thoughts-set, irrespective of the situation or event, will allow you to consider for your capabilities and skills. Develop the potential to influence others to be extra high quality. Having a splendid outlook has severa notable effects. Give the area the 'present of happiness' via using awakening in your real self. By praising this exquisite nature and the human race, you could spread happiness, pleasure, and want. Being serene and calm will assist you to specific your right emotions.

It's critical to recollect that air of mystery is not a trait we certainly inherit; as an alternative, it is a gadget that humans go through. The key to developing appeal is education self-competence - the art of being able to do what desires to be finished with out being demanding or ruffled. Successful charisma requires real exercise. It calls for questioning and feeling like you are on a degree with different humans. In different terms, you want to don't forget that being a attraction is a talent that includes time and exercising.

You'll need to paintings in your manners, apprehend how others sense, and use your appeal at its maximum and maximum strong functionality. Practice permitting others to feel unfastened to pry information out of you, supply sincere exams, and ask questions. This will let you sense extra assured and on-undertaking on the equal time as geared up to reply to invites to dinner or lunch along side your colleagues.

Make a power of intelligence – hold your intelligence quotient immoderate via retaining updated with contemporary activities and obtaining effective popular expertise abilties. Always start conversations with expert understanding thru portraying your mind in a way that the target market can with out problems apprehend, adapt, and end up engrossed in. Make an try to recognize a hint bit about a large kind of topics and areas.

Never restriction your understand-the way to a unmarried location of know-how; as a substitute, make bigger your horizons. Act assertively via encouraging others to transport in the proper path. Combining with powerful cognitive intelligence, being emotionally wise is crucial for attracting charismatic humans. Our success, leadership, relationships, intellectual nicely-being, and physical health are all inspired through our intelligence. Five factors may be used to broaden air of thriller, all of which is probably co-related to intelligence. They are as follows:

- Self-Awareness

- Motivation

- Self-Management

- Social Skills

- Empathy

The Components of a Charismatic Mind

A charismatic thoughts-set is a way of thinking - centered on the immoderate first-rate and inspirational. People with a charismatic attitude accept as true with that there may be usually something to be gained from each enjoy and that the entirety can be advanced. They are superb and trust that whatever is possible. They are also pretty assured of their skills and regularly take motion with out hesitation. These abilities make people herbal leaders and motivators.

Power is the middle of the so-called air of secrecy attitude. According to John French and Bertram Raven, of the maximum important psychologists of the 50s, there are five bases of electricity that assist one exude air of mystery, and those are:

Reward

Charismatic humans are not tremendous, however they make certain that they make up for some issue they lack. For example, Kate isn't a royal, but it have become as even though she didn't experience the same issues that the past due Princess Diana had. She knew the manner to in shape right in. She knew a way to be herself at the same time as though being capable of be part of the royal family, and for this reason, many human beings look up to her for it.

Authenticity

People who have air of thriller are by no means no longer as exact as others. They recall human beings will look as an entire lot as them, and further they consider that thru being who they may be, humans will come what may be obedient and love them the way they will be.

Strong Perception of Oneself

This stems from someone's "perceived" beauty and the sensation that he's worth of others' admiration.

Convincing

A charismatic person with out issues makes others recognize what he believes in, and receives the ones people to paintings for the same reason he's searching for to gain.

Being an Expert

Even in case you're now not super at a few aspect, you accept as real with you can do it. Does this imply which you additionally should be boastful by using being charismatic? No, not definitely. It most effective technique which you might no longer permit humans placed you down and make you experience like you're lots less than you are - and that might accomplish that a notable deal in your very very own character!

The Building Blocks of Charisma

To placed it clearly, you need to apprehend that certain building blocks make air of thriller what it is. These are:

• You want to have appropriate self-self perception

• You need to have appropriate social skills

• You need to have the potential to influence others

• You need to have first rate conversation abilties

• You want to have strong frame language

• You want to be real and real

• You want to learn how to be extra magnetic/likable

The ones said above are the very foundation, and those are people who we may be walking on in the course of this e-book. However, it's far constantly an advantage if you have any of the capabilities beneath!

• Having a revel in of force/reason

- The passion for assembly humans and supporting others revel in properly

- A ardour for studying

- A ardour for telling testimonies

- A passion for facts others and placing yourself of their shoes

- Having verbal swagger

- Having a presence and understanding the right frame language

What it Takes to be Charismatic?

There isn't always one method to this query as one-of-a-type people are manifestly charismatic in one in all a kind techniques. However, there are some not unusual elements that most a success charismatics percentage. First, they may connect to humans on a non-public diploma. They actually have a deep sense of conviction and can deliver this message convincingly to others. Finally, they're capable of encourage and inspire others to movement.

The following are a number of the center elements that you want to need to be considered "charismatic."

Purpose

People will look at your example in the occasion that they trust you have got a cause for doing so. No one will look at a person who does not apprehend wherein they will be going. Leaders are armed with a street map. If they do no longer, their proper-hand man takes care of factors. When they talk, they do now not stutter or stumble over their phrases. They make sure that their message is received efficaciously and that the listeners recognize exactly what they're pronouncing. A charismatic character will by no means lose sight of his or her enjoy of cause. This is the first and maximum vital element you have to recognize in case you need to gain humans's admire and self guarantee in you.

Mystery

If you keep people guessing about what's going on to your head, they will usually look out for what you're going to do. Soap opera writers recognize this. That is why tv collection art work. They maintain the goal marketplace on their toes. Why not be a residing cleansing soap opera, giving human beings what they need, most effective to pull again because it's now not but time for them to recognize the actual deal.

Men like mysterious women. For them, it's far a pastime to get to understand someone. If they have a look at the entirety approximately the woman at once, there may be now not whatever left to the creativeness. To be charismatic, you want to preserve an air of thriller round you. When you communicate, don't inform an excessive amount of about your self. Keep private subjects non-public, and, if there have to be a need to inform a non-public be counted, don't spill all of the data. Make the opposite person ask questions because this indicates they have got turn out to be curious, and you've got got were given end up thrilling. Keep human beings at arm's duration, in order that they wouldn't be able to parent you out that resultseasily.

On the alternative hand, it might moreover be better if you hint on the uncanny. Having an air of mystery of psychic objects will constantly be charismatic for people. If you're watching for subjects with authority on your voice, it is probably that human beings will think it to be real and will take your words as interest.

Eloquence

Nothing enhances your charismatic character more than your command of the English language. Politicians and orators of the great superb are well aware of this reality. A charismatic character can connect with others through the electricity of phrases. Words are the quickest and only manner of causing an emotional disturbance. You can call into question prison tips alongside side your terms. You is probably able to guard a person in court docket in case you communicate their language. You might be able to wiggle your way out of a brilliant vicinity certainly through the usage of the right terms. Everyone who meets you may fast understand that you're fabricated from difficult stuff and function the wits to suit your air of mystery.

Vulnerability

Display a want for affection and love. Be open for your target audience. Too an awful lot self notion ruins the facade, but you get to win humans to your facet after they see you to your prone usa. Crying may be the ideal route, but it is also the lamest. To be inclined as a charismatic man or woman, you should be open to receiving love. Be open to the human beings spherical you who need to surround you with love and affection.

Passion

Actors who play their roles passionately win awards. Athletes who need to train tough and beautify their talents continuously garner the maximum wins. You want to do some thing which you absolutely love and unleash your passion, regardless of what others think. If your ardour is writing, for example (like me!), display the world how an entire lot you need to pursue this irrespective of events.

Magnetism

The handiest manner to attract people toward you is to maintain your eyes open all of the time. It is vital to preserving eye touch with the alternative character while speaking. When you ask someone for a pick, use your eyes to talk your request. The eyes can do one factor, and the mouth can perform a little aspect definitely one-of-a-kind. Both want to collaborate to obtain success. Attempting to make someone like you will be a success if you appearance the person within the eyes and smile. Being authoritative is similar to being charismatic - you look intently at the target audience before announcing the best terms. Keep your gaze constant on the problem and workout making your eyes reflect what you are pronouncing. People also can see via your eyes and hit upon even as someone is mendacity to themselves.

Can Charisma be Learned?

Charisma is not a natural trait; as an alternative, it develops via social interactions. Few human beings are born with, or very own, these supernormal traits, but sure personality trends could make a few humans greater charismatic than others.

Yes, due to the fact air of mystery is a potential that can be determined out as opposed to inherited. Some human beings exude air of mystery, giving the effect that they've been born with those tendencies, but charisma also can be considered as a behavior, not handiest a trait.

Because air of mystery may be observed and advanced, nearly every body willing to position in the effort and time can develop charismatic behaviors by listening to human beings they consider are charismatic, studying from them, and adapting those developments.

Chapter 7: What Are The Characteristics Of A Charismatic Person?

There's no denying that charismatic people are some of the maximum a achievement human beings. Professor Wiseman of the University of Hertfordshire in the United Kingdom believes that charisma is 50% innate and 50% determined via enjoy. The maximum crucial additives of air of mystery are simple moves that, with time and repetition, emerge as ingrained for your persona and enhance your interactions with anyone spherical you, thereby increasing your normal pleasure with lifestyles and well-being.

They Actively Participate in Conversations

Give them your undivided hobby on the same time as you pay interest, and do no longer be afraid to ask questions. Avoid checking your cellphone more than as soon as during a conversation - better yet, avoid checking it in any respect! According to a check finished through the University of Colorado, active listening permits avoid misunderstandings and opens human beings as lots due to the fact the opportunity of saying greater. The capability to actively pay hobby will help you talk more correctly with the ones on your immediately surroundings, whether or now not or now not you are operating with them or dwelling with them. Positive humans are more likely to be remembered at the identical time as they'll be true listeners.

They Speak Clearly and Confidently

Take it sluggish and recollect every sentence cautiously. The extra you operate useless filler in your speech, the lots less smooth your message is. Practice your method before speaking to a set of people, mainly on the same time as talking to a couple of individual at a time or to a brand new institution of people. Is the whole thing I need to mention popping out in a single sentence? What I'm pronouncing now, do you think it is important? Can you turn out to be privy to a easy purpose and purpose for what I'm pronouncing?

They Take Their Stand

Consider the following situation: a string is going for walks from your navel, via your head, and up into the ceiling of your room. An vintage dancer's trick additionally works for the rest human beings to hold our posture in test inside the course of the day. Good posture offers the impact that you are regular and assured; if you aren't feeling confident nowadays, fake like you are till you are! Keep your shoulders as low as viable whilst gambling.

They Always Express Their Gratitude

Have you ever heard the phrase "It's no longer what you are pronouncing, it's far the way you assert it?" If you're required to critique someone, reflect onconsideration on the manner you would really like to be critiqued in advance than you begin. Keep it clean and to the factor. Address the difficulty handy and advocate an answer. Gather feedback and installation a timetable. Give credit score and compliments to folks who deserve them on the equal time as remaining expert. Make others enjoy crucial after they deserve it with the beneficial aid of expressing your appreciation for a finished venture or a presentation that went properly. Building your very very very own self-self warranty is crucial, but being capable of inspire others to do the same is what air of mystery is all about.

They Can Remember Names

According to Dale Carnegie, a legendary a success author and author who changed into referred to as "Mr. Charisma" himself, "A character's name is to him or her the sweetest and maximum vital sound in any language." It's trustworthy, but it is effective. When you first have a have a look at a person's name, say "Hi Amanda" or "It's a pride to satisfy you, Amanda" lower decrease returned to them to permit them to understand you have got were given got heard their call. Also, at the identical time as you are finished with the conversation, say their call. It will help a extraordinary deal.

They Make Perfect Eye Contact

Maintain eye contact with the individual that is speakme to you. Eye touch is one of the most critical factors of conversation as it lets in you to see for yourself whether or not or no longer or now not your message is being received successfully. It keeps the opposite individual's hobby on you and your hobby on the opposite individual's terms and because of this. You need to make one aspect of eye contact with as many humans inside the target audience as viable even as giving a presentation or speech. It will assist your intention marketplace experience a wonderful deal more associated with the event.

Chapter 8: Understand The Different Types Of Charisma

The capability to speak efficiently is the maximum crucial talent you may analyze. To be smooth, it is a knowledge each person can analyze. Throughout records, every incredible and now not-so-fantastic leaders have used charisma to steer their followers, apprehend the needs of others, and construct accept as true with.

Everyone has a natural tendency toward unique sorts of air of mystery, and this tendency adjustments sooner or later of our lives relying on our personalities and existence stories. Which ones ring a bell with you? Furthermore, which of them do you observed you can make better?

The suitable information is that you may emerge as extra gifted at the use of them with a touch little little bit of practice. It won't be smooth, however as with anything honestly nicely well worth carrying out, the attempt pays off handsomely in the end in your interpersonal relationships.

Focus

You most likely have a chum with whom you experience cushty discussing your issues. They are absolutely present and attentive to each word you assert, allowing you to sense valued and respected. People are more likely to consider which you recognize and understand their emotions if you task a robust experience of interest.

What is the super manner to increase recognition and charisma? By making sturdy eye contact with people, every even as speakme to them and while being spoken to, once in a while nodding to permit them to apprehend you are listening, and the usage of terms together with "Yes" and "I recognize," you can set up a true connection with them. The key proper here is presence – giving your complete interest to the person you're speakme with.

Visionary

Consider the likes of Steve Jobs and Martin Luther King Jr. Leaders who had a vision for the destiny and will persuade others to percent that vision, and who were exceptionally charismatic. People have been interested by them thru their bold conviction and fervent belief in their vision. People are honestly terrified of the unknown and cling to people with a pastime plan.

Visionary air of mystery is advanced via growing a robust vision and talking that imaginative and prescient to others in a manner that conjures up them. You want to be absolutely assured in your capability to supply the message. With the responsibility transfer, you may placed an save you to your self-doubt. Close your eyes, take three deep breaths, and visualize lifting the weight of your worries off your shoulders and passing it without delay to a benevolent entity.

Kindness

Do you comprehend those parents which can be brimming with fine energy and unfold love wherever they pass? That's what kindness and air of mystery are all approximately. The capability to generate magnetic warmth in others to motive them to enjoy welcome and wellknown is essential for constructing relationships. You must have compassion and goodwill inside the direction of others in your coronary coronary heart.

The maximum critical issue of growing kindness air of mystery is to pay attention to one's body language. Negative and closed-off body language must be avoided in any respect charges. Mirroring the alternative character's body language will assist you installation take transport of as real with and encourage them to speak in self belief to you. Adapt the pitch and tone of your voice to healthy theirs.

Authority

Because of our natural instincts to examine authority, authority is the most effective shape of air of mystery, this is the exceptional. The international's greatest leaders, every correct and terrible, have persuaded others that they can trade the route of records. Although growing authority air of mystery will no longer make you extra likable, it'll assist you in number one your organization.

Your body language need to be dominant, your actions gradual and comfortable, and your movements have to show that you may walk the walk. Take up quite some bodily region and speak at a decrease pitch than maximum human beings. When you preserve your cool, calm, and accumulated demeanor, you will exude authority and self-guarantee to the ones spherical you.

Even the garments you placed on can exude authority. When you placed on a properly-kept in form, it communicates that you are extreme about your process. It communicates to others that you may manage to pay for to put on steeply-priced clothing and which you are doing something proper an outstanding way to carry out that.

Everyone possesses a sure quantity of air of secrecy that comes manifestly, whilst others are extra tough to control. It takes time and effort to come to be proficient in every kind and take a look at them correctly to your private and expert lifestyles.

Chapter 9: Why Should You Consider Developing Your Charisma?

Charisma is one of the maximum essential dispositions you could very personal. It units you aside from your pals, providing you with the capability to connect to those round you and inspire them to obtain not unusual dreams. Charisma can also be used to get earlier for your profession, and it can be a valuable tool at the same time as interacting with others. There are many motives why you want to expand air of mystery, so do not wait any similarly and begin operating on enhancing your abilities nowadays!

The ability to encourage others is one of the maximum important traits a frontrunner might also have. In addition to distinguishing you out of your friends, it gives you the ability to connect with the ones in your immediately location and inspire them to gather not unusual desires. Charisma additionally can be used to bolster in your professional existence, and it is able to be a beneficial device while interacting with others in giant. There are severa reasons why you want to paintings on growing your air of mystery, so do no longer placed it off any similarly and get to artwork on enhancing your skills proper away!

When you forestall to recall it, it's miles extremely tough to perform whatever substantial in life. The more the quantity of people inclined to help you, the less complex and additional a achievement a while on this planet could be. As if by way of magic, being charismatic attracts the eye of others, attracting those who are inclined to manual you on your endeavors and who agree with within the values you constitute. It additionally assists you in getting what you need out of situations even as remaining the first rate man, making it an important person trait to cultivate – a sort of essential existence capability.

There is also the benefit of getting higher relationships because it makes us revel in better approximately ourselves. When we apprehend and understand our individuality (more on that during a 2d) and end up extra snug in various conditions, we're more likely to attain our complete ability and experience confident in any state of affairs. That approach we can take gain of the opportunities that gift themselves in a manner that we might now not be able to do if we have been specializing within the gap among ourselves and others in choice to at the bonds that could be fashioned.

You have a wealth of statistics and capabilities, and it seems the type of waste that they will be now not being positioned to finish use due to the reality you're unsure of a way to specific yourself. I understand that it seems to be counterintuitive, however someone brave and willing to take a threat truely makes us revel in extra secure. In situations in which they may be in advance human beings, in vicinity of at the back of us, we are much more likely to consider them due to the truth we gravitate toward folks that embody the trends that we would love to look in ourselves.

You won't be capable of envision your self as a splendid chief, and you can no longer even choice to be one. To gain achievement, there can be no want to visit extremes, collectively with turning into a politician or employer wealthy individual. Developing gravitas and have an impact on to attract others on your aspect of view in order that they assist you and need you to prevail is all that is required proper here.

Chapter 10: Exploring The Three Core Components Of Charisma

Individuals with charismatic personalities are tremendously powerful. They can be the chief of the unfastened international, however this does not always suggest that they're additionally the chairman of a primary multinational organisation. In reality, people who embody electricity can be located in even the humblest of instances. "Being perceived as having the capability to have an impact on the sector spherical us," says Cabane, "Means being perceived as having the functionality to affect the sector round us, whether through impact on or authority over others, huge sums of coins, information, intelligence, sheer physical strength, or immoderate social popularity," he says.

Being capable of have an effect on our environment. Powerful humans can get subjects finished, or as a minimum, they provide the affect that they're able to. People are drawn into the orbit of charismatic human beings like a magnet, and electricity is on the coronary coronary heart of that magnetic stress. It's a primal enchantment, to position it mildly. We have to have survived if we have been excellent with the large puppies on the pinnacle of the social hierarchy, who may moreover need to provide us with protection, food, and lady companionship in our caveman days. Our brains have advanced to select up on frame language and status markers that suggest electricity to higher assist us in searching out and latching onto such humans.

We ought to emphasize that each of the 3 components of air of mystery should be skillfully mixed to offer private magnetism. This is fantastically vital to remember. Your presence and heat may be the most affable and attentive man or woman within the room, but if you do not have strength, people will see you as nothing more than a pleasant man or woman, or worse, as a person decided and in want of help. It can also moreover seem harsh, however the rate humans region for your presence and heat is largely dependent on the quantity of power they recognize you to have.

The mixture of all three elements results in charismatic conduct.

Presence

Isn't it actual that we instinctively understand while a person is absolutely present with us? Even despite the reality that we won't be consciously aware of it, we revel in strong about them. The truth that someone appreciates us will boom our chance of doing the same for them because of our natural tendency to want to reciprocate. In the identical way, at the same time as a person directs all in their electricity toward us, we are capable of direct all of our electricity in the course of them, growing the possibility that we will leave with a first rate impact of them fixed in our minds. My spouse will on occasion say something like, 'That's a pleasant person; I'll hold him in thoughts.'

On the other hand, hold in mind the manner you experience whilst you are speakme to someone whose eyes are darting round or whose smile abruptly disappears from their face. Their presence for you is faded due to their failure to offer you their entire hobby. You have a nagging feeling that a few thing is wrong, but you can not positioned your finger on what it is. Because part of your mind constantly monitors what is going on, it isn't always feasible to loosen up and revel in the conversation. We have a critical human choice to sense strong, so whilst a person makes us sense uncomfortable, we want to break out from them as quickly as viable.

You can see how having a sturdy presence in a group of humans is a crucial element of charismatic conduct. Furthermore, presence has a sturdy connection to the kind of air of mystery this is focused, as we mentioned in advance. Suppose you have a rather clean time focusing. In that case, you'll find out that growing a sense of presence will come pretty with out issues to you.

The Dalai Lama and former President, Bill Clinton, are famous examples of people who exude charismatic presence. Both men are truly immersed within the present 2d with the ones they're in touch with.

Power

When you have got aura, you're perceived as someone who might also have an impact on the people and sports for your lifestyles.

There are severa techniques in which people can exude energy. The evaluation may be made in terms of their physical length and strength, social reputation, financial wealth, or understanding. Like presence, being inside the presence of a person who is benevolently effective allows us to actually lighten up and experience their agency.

There's an splendid danger that you have more energy than you apprehend; if you're an professional for your issue or apprehend greater about some difficulty that subjects to others than they do, that's a deliver of strength. The secret's to demonstrate to those round you which you are willing to area your knowledge to artwork for them via using matching your knowledge with the perfect frame language and tone of voice. Charismatically effective humans constantly find time for others; thru demonstrating that you're willing to put your recognize-the way to paintings inside the issuer of your colleagues, you are correctly announcing, 'My strength poses no hazard to you due to the reality I need that will help you.'

This technique that electricity and presence need to be mixed for us to be happy of the charismatic man or woman's hobby. When became the final time you observed an actor who become truely going through the motions at some point of a communicate show interview? They can also exude an air of authority, however their lack of interest inside the issue undermines any have an impact on they might in any other case have.

It is vital now not to fall into the entice of believing that charismatic strength is ready getting the higher of others. When a person makes a huge deal about their energy, it is also due to the fact they're feeling insecure in their very own pores and pores and skin (air of thriller entails being snug for your personal pores and skin).

A robust hyperlink exists among electricity and every the visionary and authority types of aura; in case you've decided which you have strengths in each of these regions, developing your strength element of aura can be a lot plenty much less hard for you than it'll be for lots others.

Barack Obama and Madonna are famous examples of individuals who exude charismatic electricity. You need to hold in thoughts that these human beings have both detractors and supporters – all facets of air of secrecy require you to suggest for what you believe in no matter what.

Warmth

Suppose you have got had been given a warmth and charismatic character. In that case, you are perceived as someone who can genuinely impact the sector, that can result in you turning into rather influential. It is carefully associated with power due to the reality it is related to persuading one of a kind people.

Warmth is likewise carefully related to the way you installation relationships with others and extend rapport. The charismatic man or woman will display their warm temperature via open and measured body actions, and through manner of talking at a pace that permits others to take part in the verbal exchange with them. It is inclusive in nature.

Imagine your self with a person you understand who's demanding and on factor at the same time as with them, and vice versa. Even although you could no longer be privy to it, your unconscious thoughts is on excessive alert; unexpected actions and a loss of relaxation are the polar opposites of heat.

A lack of perfectionism is needed to deliver warm temperature, and one manner to carry out this is thru communique. Suppose you're at a networking event, as an example. In that case, you may address human beings to demonstrate that you're inside the identical boat as them – unsure of who to speak to and feeling a little nervous about assembly new people. This makes you more approachable and lets in you to illustrate your warmness air of thriller with them.

When it involves air of thriller, warmth is strongly associated with the kindness and recognition styles of air of mystery, so in case you've obtained non-public comments indicating that you're strong in those regions, developing a warmly charismatic individual might be a natural improvement for you.

People with charismatic warmth include Oprah Winfrey and Stephen Fry, more than one famous examples. Both are enormously a achievement those who do now not try to painting themselves as perfect and, rather, gift themselves as inclusive and approachable.

Chapter 11: What Do You Need To Have A Charismatic Attitude?

Charisma is someone pressure, gravitas, or non-public presence. Charismatic people are much more likely to be observed, followed, and revered. Previously, obtaining tendencies together with data, air of thriller, information, and management have been reserved for society's elite but, on this factor in time, the entirety appears to be approachable. Ordinary humans can now accumulate greatness.

Everything is now indoors acquire, and becoming charismatic isn't always out of the query. It is no longer regarded as a prestigious schooling or a divine gift. If you want to be a group leader, teacher, entrepreneur, political leader, or possibly a ordinary individual, you want to enlarge charismatic skills.

Charismatic stress is an imperative trait of human character that may be measured, evolved, and understood. Charisma now not handiest affects our social and expert dreams, however it's additionally critical for retaining interpersonal individuals of the family which embody parenting, mating, and relationship. Charismatic humans appear a chunk 'magical,' but their assertiveness, notion, warmth, and self perception purpose them to sincere, likable, and appealing. But, the good information is that charismatic behavior and tendencies that enchantment to others may be acquired, and all people can be charismatic. There are a few suggestions which can be essential to growing this endearing charismatic mind-set:

Have a Strong Body Language

The maximum critical elements of air of secrecy are presence and frame language. Warmth, likability, and electricity can all be conveyed thru quality body language. Standing right away collectively together along with your head held excessive demonstrates manage, electricity, and self perception. Show a wonderful mindset in all factors of your existence. Paying interest to the individual and scenario you are worried in is every other element of frame language. Keep your movements and gestures centered and your thoughts from wandering. Learn the manner to pay attention actively. Maintain vigilance and application constantly.

On the alternative hand, correct sufficient listening is finished with an open thoughts and with out judgment. To display your interest, flash a actual smile and make assertive gestures. Actively take part in any conservation try, and be obsessed on it. These minor records, if integrated, have to make you greater attractive and aid within the formation of robust bonds with others.

Create a Positive Atmosphere

Make certainly absolutely everyone enjoy special and wonderful. Helping others find out their goals with the resource of lifting their power stages is a exquisite manner to boom air of mystery. Create a pleasing environment that entices human beings in the path of it. Provide alliance to people quite absolutely along side your very personal expertise. Sincere praise and humble gratitude are a great combo to reap air of mystery. Adopt sincerity for your moves and phrases. Displaying actual behavior for different human beings is a trait of charismatic human beings. Develop a dependancy of interrogating thrilling and insightful questions and screen empathy to set up a deeper bond.

Improve Your Emotional Intelligence

Charisma and appropriate emotional intelligence are inseparable. Maintaining an emotional reference to self-popularity is a characteristic shared with the resource of a achievement people. Emotions should be saved beneath manage to make higher connections and understand others. Demonstrate empathy thru your actions and deeds. Sort your consciousness through making others revel in comfortable. An emotional connection is the vicinity to start for better levels of rapport and deeper connections. Speaking with conviction provides coloration to the verbal exchange with the aid of way of manner of various the quantity, tone, rhythm, and pitch of your voice.

Strengthen Your Self-Confidence

Boost your vanity and assertiveness. Set and then benefit small, treasured goals that will help you extend and foster your strengths. Develop some public talking skills to preserve your self assurance in public places. Identify your non-public powers and use them with dignity, respect, and kindness. A charismatic character believes of their abilities, has conviction, and is self-assured. It is crucial to dispose of shyness. Being formidable and determined is essential for air of mystery. When you actively pay attention to motivational speeches, it is easy to increase self guarantee.

Build a Charismatic Mindset

The proper form of thoughts-set is a key to developing air of thriller acquired through shaping and developing your very personal thoughts-set. Cultivate and painting humility. Humility is a gesture of our strength. It makes a person persuasive as it mushrooms honesty and braveness to combat for every different proper. Be a hint inquisitive and increase childlike interest; you'll by using threat growth connections with human beings. Always keep your self sudden, unpredictable, and mysterious. You would love an intruding man or woman's hobby, admiration, and interest. Display warm temperature and affection as it depicts you as approachable. Depict a experience of gratitude because it brings internal peace and information. A charismatic attitude as a result develops magic in you that opens an entire new worldwide of opportunity, admiration, and recognize.

Love Yourself

Remember to take real care of your self. How are you able to expect others to love you in case you do not love your self? Our unconscious thoughts sends out many signs to others about how we treat ourselves. Remember that the Almighty created us with love and affection and that we are all treasured and particular in our non-public approaches. Self-complaint has a self-defeating tendency. On the alternative hand, self-criticism has the functionality to go away us distraught and powerless, whereas self-compassion generates inner electricity and empowerment.

Learn How to Speak With Beauty

Always use implementing phrasing with a touch of polite and clever language. Highlight the notable aim and neglect about any terrible feedback. Try to provide compliments generously as they uplift arrogance and make you connected with human beings. Maintain suitable timing and difficulty compliments creatively. Express attraction together with your terms. Accept the compliments generously, irrespective of if they may be intended with contempt. Avoid the addiction of gossiping and appreciate others for their notable trouble. Be type-hearted and preserve all of us's reputation and dignity.

Chapter 12: Developing Your Confidence (Four Days)

Confidence is some detail that everybody dreams, and it is some factor that we will without difficulty come across in others. The task of summoning our very very personal self assurance, then again, can appear like an insurmountable task. The true data is that this experience of self-guarantee isn't always as elusive as it is able to appear. There are numerous strategies to boosting one's arrogance.

Where Does Self-Confidence Come From?

Confidence is a sense of self-warranty in a single's abilties, alternatives, and values. It emanates from inside you, and has the advent and revel in of an internal understanding of your very personal strengths and weaknesses, at the same time as remaining advantageous about yourself.

Self-self guarantee is derived from the information and mind we collect through our interactions with the outside worldwide that make contributions to a excellent mind-set approximately ourselves. Consider the younger infant who is self-confident and willing to take dangers, inclusive of jumping off the swings or dancing without being involved in front of a set of humans. When a younger little one is affirmed and recommended, he or she develops a more potent sense of self and starts offevolved offevolved to form cognitive schemas that verify that they are really worth, precious, cute, smart, and so on.

While many people have a robust sense of self-assurance as youngsters, existence regularly throws curve balls that could cause self guarantee to be eroded over the years. Low self-self perception can appear as an incapacity to cope with unique humans's criticisms or as a loss of self warranty in one's very own capabilities and those of others.

The superb detail is that every 2nd offers an opportunity to accumulate proof that contributes to yourself-self belief. To make up for the loss, you can step by step rebuild self guarantee via small and large reviews that growth to greater self-notion and believe through the years.

Notably, no matter performing to be synonymous on the floor, being shy or introverted does not imply a loss of self-self assurance. Shyness is a character trait wherein a few people are without a doubt reserved in social conditions. The persona trait of being an introvert end up first defined with the resource of Carl Jung as someone who prefers to show inward, to their internal worldwide, to gain readability and perception. On the opposite hand, extroverts opt to have interaction with one-of-a-kind humans and are more social.

What Are the Root Causes of Low Self-Esteem?

Just as there are topics so one can assist you to collect amazing self-self warranty, subjects can detract from it. Several factors, together with the way humans are socialized and perceived via using those round them and tough transitions through formative years, kids, and maturity, can all contribute to a loss of self-self assurance.

Some of the elements that may contribute to a negative experience of self are as follows:

• Parents who're overly crucial or reprimand their youngsters.

• Caregivers who restrict a infant's ability to discover.

• Being rejected by means of way of 1's friends.

• Transitioning right right into a built idea of "adulthood" offers demanding situations.

• Media representations and data from across the area approximately what constitutes "great" tendencies in someone.

In addition, one-of-a-kind ranges of self belief can appear themselves in exclusive situations. You may additionally additionally furthermore have advanced a strong enjoy of mathematical self perception because of your socialization and encouragement to excel in your instructional research. For example, expect you have got formerly obtained criticism from buddies and have now not but processed their comments in a useful manner. In that case, you could enjoy plenty much less confident approximately public speakme.

The accurate information is that low self-self perception may be conquer, and you're totally liable for bringing approximately this variation.

Different Ways To Boost Your Self-Confidence

Identify the Source of Your Lack of Self-Esteem

Finding the underlying reasons of low self-self perception can offer a road map for undertaking more tiers of awesome self-self belief. Self-contemplated photograph and journaling are splendid methods to get started out out on this device.

Try the following exercising that will help you pick out out the viable root cause of your lack of self-warranty:

• Over one week, jot down any horrible self-self belief mind or statements that preserve arising for you.

• In response to each belief or declaration, inquire as to "Who or what informed you that?"

• At this stage of your lifestyles, you want to decide whether or now not or not or not you need to offer that voice the authority to direct your mind.

• Write down your emotions and reactions in a magazine, and then expand a route of movement to move ahead.

• If you are having hassle with this, going for walks with a therapist or train to understand and redecorate unhelpful low-self-self perception thoughts can be useful.

Embrace How it Would Feel Like to Have Self-Confidence

Take a while to find out what it seems like to trust for your very own frame. "How will even as you've got reached a extremely good stage of self-self perception?" is a outstanding query. Perhaps you may start to talk up more frequently at paintings. You also can ultimately get to place on that outfit you have got got desired to area on. You could in all likelihood even run into your ex-boyfriend or ex-woman friend at your co-running location. As every person's mindset will variety from the following, there can be no requirement that it's going to make experience to anyone else. You can use this to gauge your very own degree of self-guarantee.

Get in Touch With Your Inner Self

You should take a step decrease returned and mirror in case you find out your self the usage of the phrase "need to" loads (for example, I have to be married with the aid of 30 years antique, have a residence via subsequent year, or have my existence collectively now). What is the supply of this "need to" declaration?

Many of the "shoulds" in a single's existence are derived from cultural or familial duties. If you are making any of these statements, it's a exquisite concept to usually ask your self, "Is this what I absolutely want for myself?"

You can take decrease once more manage of your life at any time. When you're making steady decisions together along with your authentic self and your dreams, you will advantage greater self assurance for your desire-making.

Take Small Steps

The majority human beings do not enjoy being subjected to a amazing deal of change. Starting small is a completely essential part of any self-development challenge.

Shirin Eskandani, lifestyles educate and founder of Wholehearted Coaching, believes that making small guarantees to yourself and following via on them is a wonderful way to build self-self assurance. "And the operative phrase right here is "small." Carry out duties which can be tough but moreover feasible for you. So, assume you aren't a morning person. In that case, you will likely remember switching to an night routine as opposed to committing to waking up at 6 a.M. Every day to do a morning normal."

Adopt a Growth Mindset

When you have were given a increase thoughts-set, you're encouraged to appearance past your current-day-day talents and statistics, while constantly keeping the possibility of improvement in thoughts. If you find yourself announcing such things as "I'm not confident," simply upload the phrase "however" to the give up of the phrase, which transforms the antique notion into "I'm now not confident however." This qualifies your announcement thru asserting that you are within the manner of reading capabilities to end up greater confident.

According to a have a have a look at published in 2019, increase mind-set interventions advanced math grades for immoderate university university college students, with the grades improving even more even as college students were immersed in environments that promoted increase attitude ideas and practices. As a end stop result, it's far profitable to talk about your new growth mind-set with others who percentage your thing of view.

Recognize That it's Completely Fine to Fail

The majority of people extremely good communicate about their accomplishments due to the fact we stay in a life-style that is frightened of failure. There are only some times wherein you may pay interest approximately humans's research with failure. Understanding that failure is inevitable and that it's far a crucial part of the manner of living will let you stay life to the fullest.

We were generally taught that self-self warranty comes from achievements for numerous us. It does advocate that after we succeed, we've got got excessive self guarantee in our abilties, however while we fail, our self-self guarantee takes a beating. In fact, I take shipping of as real with that self-self notion stems from our very personal ideals approximately our non-public abilties, rather than from outside achievements or accomplishments, so that we're able to preserve our self-self guarantee no matter whether or not or no longer we gain achievement or fail.

Don't Listen to Your Inner Critic

Sometimes it is tough to place your religion in yourself because of the reality you have got obtained critical feedback from authority figures earlier in lifestyles, along with mother and father, teachers, or network leaders, and you've have been given internalized their criticisms as your personal. However, there comes the factor at which this feedback isn't beneficial on your cutting-edge situation. Standing as an awful lot as the ones antique criticisms will let you advantage a newfound feel of self-assure.

The ability to assemble self belief also may be completed with the aid of rewriting the narratives that we have in our heads approximately our worthiness. This involves figuring out and reframing self-proscribing beliefs, amongst diverse matters. Often, the voice in our heads that tells us we aren't fantastic enough is not our right voice however as an opportunity an amalgamation of all the voices of those who've criticized us inside the beyond and are though judging us. The confident inner little one we've got were given misplaced touch with can re-emerge if we communicate over again to the internal critic for an extended sufficient time.

Appreciate That Emotions Are Temporary

Emotions go through a 3-stage cycle: a starting, a middle, and an end. Although emotions can be extremely severe within the suggest time, they'll be simplest there for a quick duration. Emotions are physiological responses to stimuli to your environment which might be uncontrollable at their most critical degree. If your WiFi is going down proper earlier than your business enterprise's presentation, you can revel in a unexpected rush of anxiety. Your sister's wonder package deal may additionally moreover purpose you to be conquer with feelings of deep happiness and gratitude. If you obtain a text from your ex, you can enjoy a warm streak of disappointment that lasts for a few moments. Whatever the stimuli and coupled emotion, they may be all statistics factors that may be used to guide your next motion step.

In phrases of self belief, any bad emotion, which includes tension, stress, or fear that forestalls you from taking movement, is best transient. Once it has subsided, you can retain to the following step. To paraphrase an vintage adage, "Feel the concern and do it besides."

Concentrate On the Aspects of Life That You Can Control

Often, we base our self-self notion on matters we don't have any manipulate over, along aspect what one of a kind humans think, the final consequences of a project, the reactions of others, and so on. To boom our self-self notion, we must permit pass of our attachment to matters we cannot manipulate and begin to base our self-self perception on matters we can manage.

When you are strolling on a presentation, as an example, one may additionally additionally recommend that you should take a destroy. Depending to your personality kind, you may area a extremely good deal of emphasis on other humans's opinions, mission effects, or the reactions of your buddies to your paintings. Our organization recommends that you deal with the factors of your presentation which you have manage over, which includes your steering, your enthusiasm for the subject, and the quantity of try you have got positioned into it. This will help you gather self-self perception in conditions which you can't control.

Making a foundation for your self in topics you can manage, even if it is just one thing of your purpose, will provide you with more self assurance and balance as you flow into forward. And preserve in thoughts that gaining self guarantee consequences in more self notion. By beginning with the subjects you may control, you may make certain that you are building self assurance from an area of inner strength in preference to outdoor power.

Chapter 13: Developing Your Social Skills (Four Days)

What makes human beings high-quality from first rate lower animals is their capability to speak via language and create friendships. Communication lets in people to meet every different's wishes and set up friendships. For a person to interact with others, they want social abilties - the capacity to apprehend how we act in society and our very own shallowness. This economic catastrophe targets to provide you beneficial tips on a way to enhance your social competencies, set goals, the importance of empathy in constructing relationships with each other or making buddies. It might also offer records approximately know-how oneself and efficiently interacting with others so that all may also moreover advantage from such know-how.

Definition and Importance of Social Skills

Social talents are the talents that help people to speak, interact and create non violent interpersonal relationships. Social interactions have an entire lot of materials, collectively with the potential to communicate, have an impact on, and collect harmonious members of the circle of relatives. There are precise degrees of verbal exchange that embody interpersonal verbal exchange, employer conversation, and social media-primarily based actually interactions, among diverse things. Communication may be grouped as written or verbal counting on whether it's far finished through symbols (written) or words (verbal). Written communications use symbols for messages, at the same time as verbal way spoken terms applied in an oral conversation with numerous nonverbals, along with gestures, to offer usually on the equal time as talking.

Social talents are massive whilst you're worried in any communique act. Having the ones abilties lets in you to have interaction with people excellently. Furthermore, people will be aware of your message at the same time as you personal social talents. There are diverse advantages of social capabilities. These encompass:

Helps Create a Friendly Environment

People with social skills can engage nicely with others, which can assist them keep away from conflicts and reduce the superiority of troubles. Leaders can understand those around them and feature a study persuasive techniques to persuade others with the ones tendencies.

More Knowledge

When you personal superb social talents, you may interact with human beings from numerous backgrounds and benefit a good buy information. The statistics that you obtain assists you in lessening battle.

Expands Your Network

When you have got social competencies, you'll be capable of talk with many humans from specific backgrounds. Some of these humans may additionally moreover gift possibilities as a manner to help enhance your economic lifestyles.

Opens Up Your Perspectives

When you personal terrific social competencies, you can provide your own perspectives on tremendous subjects. These perspectives can also help extraordinary people.

Helps Stay Focused

With social skills, you could get focused on achieving shared dreams.

Qualities That Enhance Social Skills

Social talents are crucial to every body who desires to be successful in lifestyles. This is because those competencies assist us to create and nurture relationships. In case you want to enhance your social abilities, there are plenty of tendencies that you have to adopt. These are as follows:

Effective Communication

Communication is an imperative part of social competencies. Communication allows you articulate your thoughts to others efficaciously and spotlight them within the technique. When you're correct at conversation, it is simpler in case you want to paintings with a team in the direction of attaining goals collectively.

Conflict Resolution

In any social environment, conflicts every so often emerge. If you're a chief with excellent social abilties, you may solve those conflicts harmoniously.

Active Listening

To pay hobby actively manner that you be aware of some factor is stated. When you're taking note of the alternative birthday party, they may respect you. There are particular strategies that you may rent to be an energetic listener. These embody: heading off distractions, concentrated on what is said, and getting nicely prepared to announcement or ask questions.

Empathy

Empathy permits you to look a state of affairs via someone else's eyes and feel their emotions. If they will be feeling satisfied, you will be satisfied for them; if they may be sad, then the very last element for your mind is probably what is making them disillusioned.

Empathetic people are eminently aware about unique humans's feelings and take care in evaluating how those emotions may additionally have an effect on themselves and others involved within the courting. Developing those skills is an extraordinary manner to form extended-lasting relationships with others. You have developed strong bonds with particular customers or customers at the same time as you manage a dating thru connecting with them.

Respect

Respect is an critical problem of conversation. When you apprehend others, you could allow them to mention subjects without interruption. When speakme, you furthermore mght understand humans with the useful resource of asking thoughtful and applicable questions, being targeted on the subject, and avoiding time wastage.

Tactics for Improving Your Social Skills

Seeking Feedback

You can decorate your social skills with the resource of asking your closest comrades and buddies to tell you of areas they count on you need to enhance. You must choose any honest remarks and use it to decorate your social abilities.

Set Goals

When you apprehend the regions of development, it is essential to formulate a plan on how you may enhance your self. In your perception, make certain that you've set unique and measurable dreams.

Find Resources

Various resources let you in improving your social competencies. These consist of using the net, analyzing applicable books, and attending particular education.

Practicing

After mastering the severa techniques for reinforcing your social talents, you need to placed what you've determined out into exercise. You can start operating towards at domestic or at artwork.

Keep Learning

The thriller to keeping improving your social skills is to preserve mastering.

How to Improve Your Empathy

Empathy is the ability to recognize with unique human beings's feelings. An empathetic man or woman can recognize every distinctive individual's feelings and offer a solution. There are severa components of empathy that you need to increase. These encompass:

Improve Your Listening Skills

An empathic person is right at listening. When you've got superb listening abilties, you do now not interrupt others even as they're speakme, ask pertinent questions, and make nicely-taken into consideration comments. People will speak in confidence to you, so learning to be empathetic is critical.

Be More Attentive

Being attentive manner paying near interest to what the opportunity person is announcing. It is quality to keep away from any distractions that prevent you from listening attentively. You need to additionally refrain from interrupting the opportunity celebration at the identical time as they may be speakme.

Appreciate the Culture of Others

When you discover ways to apprehend awesome human beings's cultures, you extend empathetic talents. This necessitates huge adventure to satisfy new humans from numerous cultural backgrounds. When you recognize why humans behave the manner they do, you becomes greater empathetic and learn how to admire them with out prejudice.

Read More Books

Reading one among a kind books explores the topic of empathy. It's vital to look for those books and take a look at them to improve your empathy skills. You can also search for valuable materials on the internet that shed mild as regards to empathy.

Evaluate Your Biases

To be empathetic, it's far crucial to take a look at the biases that we've got about others, which prevents us from being attentive to them empathetically. Maybe you're biased towards any individual due to their race, colour, or gender. When you dispose of those biases, you'll beautify your empathetic abilties.

Always be Curious

When you are curious, you need to take note of one-of-a-kind humans's reminiscences no matter their heritage. This interest will can help you beautify your empathy due to the truth you'll take time to be aware of people you'll in no way have heard within the first region.

Ask the Right Questions

The type of questions you ask will determine the quantity of empathy you can display. It's essential to discover ways to ask the proper questions applicable to the problem below dialogue.

Steps to Getting New Friends

You're in all likelihood to fulfill new faces most of the time. It's crucial to increase competencies on how we need to start, nurture, and enlarge new relationships. This segment gives you pointers on a way to make new friends.

Don't be Afraid

Some people are concerned about meeting new humans. They'll spend a long term brooding about what they will tell those new people and what impressions they'll form of them. In other phrases, the opportunity of assembly new people is concerned. However, it's miles vital to understand that your fear is unfounded and handiest serves to keep new friends from entering into your existence.

Start Small

Suppose you're afraid of meeting in reality new humans with whom you'll socialize and emerge as right buddies with. In that case, it's satisfactory initially people . In this regard, it is vital to begin with your friends and buddies and take shipping of invites to go out. Starting with humans will help you growth self-self belief in assembly people you have by no means met in advance than in your life.

Explore More

After you have got strengthened your friendship ties together along with your inner circle, it's time to challenge out and meet absolutely new people. Meet-ups, workshops, volunteering, going to sports and clubs, and distinct activities assist you to attain this purpose. Meet-up organizations will can help you meet individuals who share your hobbies. You should, for instance, installation a meet-up of individuals who are interested by cycling or online advertising and advertising. Workshops provide education opportunities for humans inquisitive about precise fields, which include studies. It's crucial to find out while a workshop that pastimes you could begin so you can attend and make new friends.

Take Your First Step

The first step is to greet and introduce yourself to a person. Tell the alternative birthday celebration what you do for your lifestyles, and then allow them to answer.

Avoid entering into complicated subjects inside the starting; instead, ask easy questions consisting of how they determined precise topics in the workshop.

Be Open-Minded

It's essential to open your mind at the identical time as you meet new faces available and keep away from the tendency to prejudge them. You must commonly permit a while skip in advance than you begin judging people. For example, if you would like a friend who loves touring to new locations however thinks that the only you've actually met doesn't, it's crucial to offer them time earlier than you begin judging them. You also can moreover arouse their interest, and they will begin wishing to tour more. In the equal breath, it's additionally essential to open your coronary heart to the opposite celebration. This manner that you begin trusting them and believing that they're your right buddies.

Chapter 14: Developing Your Influence

Sometimes we need to persuade others, however it can be tough. Whether at work or definitely round humans in contemporary, one manner to installation a courting is through our private management abilties. Anyone can turn out to be a frontrunner - all that subjects is the take into account of those they're searching for to manual and their ability no longer to govern them. Becoming a pacesetter isn't always smooth; from time to time, you've got accurate attributes and may supply in your ensures however fail because of the reality others soak up too much space, like while someone has greater electricity over one of a kind humans than you do (as judged thru voting).

Influence is the capability to trade a person's mind, selections, and moves. The definition can sound not possible, but it's miles viable if you are a top notch leader. Influence in the fundamental way compliance - making a person do what you want them to undertake together along with your needs.

All round us, we will see the effect of exchange - and that is have an impact on. The capability to make new pals or art work with humans correctly with none authority determines whether an individual can be a success in his dreams, motivations, and inspirations while ensuring that they will be normally on their aspect. The difficult component approximately this control approach lies in having no manipulation worried the least bit; it's a measurable, predictable, and repeatable detail.

Types of Influence

Negative Influence

This is the polar opposite of first-rate have an impact on and is commonly the maximum detrimental type due to the fact individuals who interact in it are particularly concerned with power or authority over others. These humans are selfish and proud, and they normally use pressure or a form of trickery to get to the pinnacle. As a give up end result, they will be leaders, however they lack understand, and people find out it difficult to have a look at and listen to them. As the name shows, their results are normally negative, hurting each the enterprise corporation or the group. These leaders, moreover, fail to reap any useful intention because of the reality the effects produced are frequently insufficient. It is essential to do away with or keep away from such leaders due to the fact their motivation for control is typically risky.

Neutral Influence

Neutral affects are a leader's favored practices and attitudes that do not have any splendid or horrible effect on others. These leaders are generally independent and have little effect, making them stand proud of the group. In one of a kind terms, they do now not upload or subtract value from an commercial enterprise agency or employer. They provide no assist, take no motion, or end up proactive. Despite having no blessings or dangers, those leaders normally sit down down down decrease again and appearance ahead to the personnel or humans under their control to do so and benefit specific dreams because of the fact they may be never encouraged. This is each different type to keep away from because the ones leaders do now not some thing to enhance their positions.

Positive Influence

Leaders are tremendous examples of excessive superb impact due to the reality they upload fee and paintings with happy people. This is a very useful have an impact on, especially for leaders who are actively concerned with human beings and function first-class movements and attitudes toward others. The terrific element of this individual kind is that the chief turns into the only who creates and grows relationships with others via belief, control, and education. Being a nice influencer way that you could fast set up yourself as a mentor and help others in turning into a fulfillment. Furthermore, this form of have an effect on necessitates better intentionality, strive, and passion for ensuring that everybody succeeds in lifestyles.

Life-Changing Influence

This is the maximum treasured and zenith kind of have an effect on, and only a few people try to accumulate it. Despite having a exceptional have an impact on, becoming a pacesetter takes years, if no longer a long term, to comprehend the competencies required to guide properly and change lives. As in the direction of splendid have an effect on, lifestyles-changing impact includes making selections that completely modify an person's life via moves or phrases. Those you've got an impact on continue to be in a comparable nation even after an organisation or group chief has exceeded away. Life-changing leaders commonly devote their complete lives, time, and interest to helping others in becoming a success, with out regard for greed, satisfaction, or the selection to meet their very personal goals. Oprah Winfrey, Mother Teresa, and Abraham Lincoln are the severa life-converting affects.

Build Relationships

Becoming a frontrunner starts offevolved with putting in accurate relationships with others, mainly while you want to make new pals. One of the methods to start an awesome courting is by technique of having a friendlier and outgoing character which typically impacts others once they locate you thrilling and snug. Be inquisitive about others without discrimination to make a super have an effect on. Address them with the useful resource in their name to make the message extra customized. Engage in open talk often, which moreover builds accept as true with. Don't strain ideas, however, as an alternative, wholesome them to subjects to hand. Share what you have got were given on the equal time as discussing different human beings's pastimes, no longer forgetting to recognize amazing opinions.

Develop Positive Reputations

Another important a part of influencing people is setting up a reputation that sticks out from the rest. This may be accomplished via manner of constantly admitting errors initially while you are incorrect and highlighting distinct human beings's wrongdoings in a logical, brilliant, indirect, and optimistic way. Besides, show your information in areas with big statistics at the same time as challenge sports activities that make humans admire and understand your way of life. You also can increase your reputation via displaying an interest in learning greater with an open thoughts, either out of your seniors or mistakes made on the way.

Support Others

As for impact, many reside on human beings; some one-of-a-kind primary step to adopt and win them over is thru presenting a helping hand in numerous methods. Among them is through drawing close to people in a friendlier manner. Never be bossy or disturbing, as this may display signs of delight and thirst for authority over others. Sympathize with the resource of displaying reciprocity on the subject of beliefs and their moves, which want to genuinely be extraordinary. Promote changes absolutely in society, at the same time as maintaining off giving commands and orders as this is generally considered disrespectful. Save people who enjoy embarrassed, at the same time as embracing folks that propose mind even as making corrections and letting those mind belong to them. Lastly, reward others as opposed to turning into jealous. Let them feel endorsed through your generosity, but by no means praise them for the advantage of creating them feel appropriate.

Different Types of Communication Style

Learning communique styles is an critical thing, specifically at the same time as leaders realise how they talk with others. It allows humans to recognize how they have interaction with friends, own family, and friends and make essential changes to have an lively and assertive interaction. The same is also crucial to people who've an effect on others; they usually have an possibility to speak and share what they have got in mind. There are one in every of a type verbal exchange patterns in which you in all likelihood can use one or greater techniques at the same time as speaking in a single-of-a-kind situations.

Assertive Style

This is the most effective communique fashion, and it's far typically utilized by leaders with hundreds better conceitedness.

It is one of the healthiest and employs all super elements of communication abilities, in conjunction with behavioral, language, verbal, and nonverbal techniques. Accepting compliments, taking obligation on your moves, popularity up in your rights at the identical time as respecting the ones of others, and expressing your self socially and emotionally are all examples of behavioral traits. This language is calm and employs nonverbal cues along with cushty, open, and symmetric posture, facial expressions, gestures, and a medium-pitched voice.

Aggressive Style

An competitive mode of conversation is whilst the speaker uses a commanding and vain tone toward others. In assessment to an assertive character, a dynamic character frequently uses a loud voice, glare, or scowling facial expressions; gestures are usually speedy and jerky, and they use postures that show they're superior to others. They are aggressive, intimidating, belligerent, demanding, and threatening. These are human beings who've a negative effect and often show pride and greed while in positions of authority. Aggressive verbal exchange normally makes the individual on the receiving stop revel in threatened, humiliated, disrespected, and uncooperative inside the verbal exchange.

Passive Style

The passive fashion is also known as passive-competitive due to the reality individuals who use it seem ordinary at the out of doors but are bitter at the interior. People who use a passive verbal exchange fashion normally will be inclined to precise their anger in distinctive techniques than thru violence and aggression. That is, folks that act on this way are powerless and resentful, and as a end result, they grow to be sabotaging themselves. Communication behavior is normally untrustworthy, sarcastic, patronizing, and includes oblique aggression. A clean and sweet voice, uneven postures, and a quick and jerky function are nonverbal behaviors.

Submissive Style

Submissive human beings are trying to find to satisfaction others to keep away from warfare, regardless of the problems they'll face in the method. This communique fashion makes others revel in greater critical and on pinnacle of things of a submissive individual. These humans often show off apologetic, opting-out, inexpressive behavior, retaining off confrontations, and feeling like a sufferer. Examples of nonverbal behaviors are fidgeting and twisting gestures, mild voices, lack of eye touch, and even though going thru down and feeling small for the duration of confrontations. People on the receiving forestall are commonly pissed off, wonderful, accountable, and exasperated.

Manipulative Style

Though no longer usually the proper verbal exchange style relevant to each person, manipulative people usually have a tendency to emerge as shrewder and scheming. This shape of communication can extensively have an impact on others, particularly folks who experience misplaced. These people regularly experience on pinnacle, and in case you attempt pushing yourself up, they end up calculative and live dominant in management positions. The language normally hides the meant which means that, making the receiving birthday party unaware of the hidden this means that portrayed. As such, manipulative people commonly tend to end up cunning, ask for subjects not right away, come to be sulking, manipulate others, and impact others to experience accountable. The voice used on this communique fashion is generally patronizing, ingratiating, and envious with unhappy and pitiful expressions.

Why Should You Understand The Styles?

As an influencer who leads specific human beings thru example, knowledge the types of communication patterns locations you on the leading fringe of learning the manner to attend to severa companies underneath your management. Depending at the situation, some will show a couple of form of communique. Understanding how they behave and feature in these situations additionally lets in you to address them correctly. As a leader, you are unfastened to apply any style, but it should be respectful, low price, and beneficial to yourself and the team or enterprise. Henceforth, learning about one-of-a-type communication styles allows you to be an terrific chief even in demanding situations.

Specific Phrases/Words to Influence Others

The English language offers the 5 most persuasive phrases that have been determined to steer humans to engage in sports and have an impact on them. However, other phrases are carried out in a unmarried-of-a-type areas, such as organisation, to inspire customers to purchase a given product. These phrases assist in persuading human beings and are also carried out in retaining manipulate positions for impact. Some of the simplest phrases used are:

And

'And' is a not unusual word used to influence humans, specifically when emphasizing unique records or products. For instance, 'you have spent a vast amount of time analyzing this e-book, and there is though hundreds to take a look at.' This approach that regardless of how a long way the reader has superior and loved the ebook, there can be even though more to find out. As a end result, you're much more likely to find out more, that you in no way predicted while you hold studying. As you parent to steer others, the word 'and' entices a reader to hold analyzing, converting his or her choice, mind, and reviews.

Because

This is every unique massive piece of hard work that offers a further rationalization of what a given piece of information or product is all about. The phrase 'because of the reality' has been used to create high-quality situations in a declaration, indicating a higher knowledge on the receiving give up. 'The grass could be very inexperienced nowadays as it rained closing week,' as an instance. In this situation, the word 'due to the fact' explains why something is the way it's far when you actually say, 'the grass can be very inexperienced in recent times.' As a end result, this phrase attempts to offer an influential ability for an character to understand the fee of a given event.

You

When you operate the phrase 'you' to seek advice from lifestyles experience, you effects separate your non-public knowledge out of your reader or goal market.

Guarantee

To convince humans in the entrepreneurial region, you need to apply extra attractive and saleable language. One of the maximum common is 'assure,' which attempts to present an reason for the brilliant and durability. This is because of the reality the market is rife with fraud, and the brilliant manner to promote products is to make assurances to customers. In this case, the time period "guarantee" became used to persuade clients to shop for a selected product primarily based totally on the information of its authenticity. However, the commercial company corporation is entire of numerous phrases to steer clients, including free, reductions, incredible, and confined.

Which Means

The word 'which means that' is likewise important for persuading humans, because it alters how they apprehend unique thoughts and beliefs. Despite sounding like a common English word, it consists of a effective message that could have an effect on the overall public to interact in a totally new interest. Furthermore, relying on how you use them, they can be used to comprehensively offer an cause behind what particular motion or mind-set is all approximately. 'You've been in this beauty for some time, which means you're analyzing some issue beneficial to your lifestyles,' for instance.

Appealing to the Audience

Influencers normally apprehend the cost in their target marketplace and use the opportunity to engage with them by means of way of manner of setting them first within the conversation. In this example, the method includes considering your target audience while making sure that they are aware of and take a look at your communicate. To impact your target market, the number one technique to utilize is to make sure that they may be positioned at the leading edge whilst highlighting your points. That is, make sure you operate the high-quality mode of communique, making your speech informative and thrilling. Appealing in your purpose market gives a higher chance of facts and related to them within the communique.

Speaking Techniques to Persuade and Influence

Utilize Nonverbal Communication Skill

Some human beings are capable of turning in a nicely-organized, savvy, and doable speech that leaves your intention marketplace happy at the side of your concern remember. When you accompany your presentation with nonverbal cues, but, you are more likely to hold your goal marketplace centered and excited. Nonverbal factors encompass famous look, emotions, gestures, and facial expressions, amongst particular subjects. The use of every verbal and nonverbal elements drives the thing domestic and guarantees that the speech is useful and brought logically. At a glance, the combination of the 2 can extensively impact greater human beings.

Use Actionable Examples

There are a few subjects that, due to their complexities, necessitate rationalization or look like not viable to deal with. As a end end result, the audience may lose awareness or understand the presentation as focusing on an no longer viable mission count with restrained concerns. In this situation, the excellent way to make it more sensible is to apply actionable examples, preferably a couple of. Furthermore, because they will be the primary goal marketplace on your speech, you may pick out to use them as pinnacle examples. Personal testimonies, experiments, and photos displayed inside the displays also are relevant examples.

Accentuate Critical Cases

Even in case you use both verbal and nonverbal factors and applicable examples, some human beings might not stay targeted and apprehend the whole lot you're saying. In this case, emphasizing key points inside the assertion is the great approach. The identical impact may be completed through pausing at every factor in which you trust the factor is vital, the usage of phrases along with 'pay attention carefully,' to emphasise the statements, and changing tone and amount in those sections. When emphasizing key points of the speech, you may moreover circulate within the path of your intention market and keep eye touch.

Involve Your Audience

To efficiently impact human beings, it is vital to allow them to make a contribution to the hassle reachable. Some people also can continue to be silent at some point of the speech with out asking or answering the query. You might also moreover fail to influence them, mainly if you fail to engage them inside the verbal exchange. You can accomplish this thru placing out a call to motion for them remarks, appealing them with destiny plans, and getting equipped a closed assembly for them to percentage their thoughts on the speech. This approach has been used by severa leaders who've successfully engaged their audiences and earned a superb popularity amongst their friends. As a end result, this approach permits you to advantage respect and keep in mind from the humans you need to persuade.

Chapter 15: Developing Your Communication Skills

Speaking talents offer all people the capability to speak correctly to those who are listening. They will let you deliver a message in a extra passionate manner that sounds convincing. The capabilities ensure the target audience will no longer misunderstand the speaker. Communication capabilities are abilities to apply at the equal time as giving and receiving statistics. Communication lets in one to be understood and recognize others. Communication skills consist of: speakme, listening, and empathizing. When speaking:

• Get your thinking proper away - complicated messages come from muddling thinking.

• Say what you imply - say your words with sincerity and reality.

• Be on aspect - get to the most critical a part of the speech. Say what you need.

- Be concise - communicate in brief and say it in acquainted phrases.

- Be real - for optimum readability, permit the real you return thru. Be natural, and you will be extra comfortable and loads extra convincing.

Incorporate an picture into your speech - a image is nicely really worth a thousand terms. You have the first-class verbal exchange at the same time as you save you, look, and pay interest.

Tactfulness - sensitive communique generally takes location in some unspecified time in the future within the speech, and it's far important to method such communication with tact whilst it takes location. Emotional intelligence is wanted at the same time as the form of period happens.

Curiosity - asking questions to the target market demonstrates that you are inquisitive about them. This is the wonderful way to installation rapport with the audience. Interest is one of the exquisite abilties for advancing your profession as it lets in you to analyze masses and accumulate new abilties. Always be open to questions and hold the communique going.

Friendliness - most human beings need to work with someone they experience comfortable with. Being courteous and cordial goes an extended way in the direction of putting in a solid and decent expert profession.

Negotiation is a whole communique in and of itself, but it's far but an crucial manner of speakme. It is a beneficial abilities to have if you want to do a remarkable procedure. For example, negotiating a income in an interview and negotiating a undertaking cut-off date. Compromise and persuasion are critical conversation capabilities.

C's of Effective Speaking

Completeness - the message want to be complete. Do not go away your intention marketplace placing. The message is geared toward the goal market's view of the area.

Concreteness – a detailed message brings approximately intense commercial enterprise employer in organization speak.

Courtesy - this suggests that you have a honest thoughts-set; it is not without a doubt politeness with a phrase like "please" and "thank you."

Correctness - the usage of correct verbal has a choice in the enterprise message. Grammatical errors need to usually be avoided. Proper use of phrases will growth honesty, and the goal market will sense that the speaker is taking them seriously.

Clarity - fuzzy language is forbidden in communique. Instead, clear language is characterized through explicitness, small sentences, and entire phrases. The target audience receives a clean image of what you are announcing by means of the use of doing this.

Consideration - the speaker considers the aim institution to whom you need to relay the message to. It's crucial to narrate to the real audience for effective communique. Factors to hold in mind whilst giving examples are the amount of schooling, expert diploma, age, and target market interest.

Conciseness - the storyline is continuously easy whilst the storyline is steady. When the factors are mentioned, it's though vital to stay everyday.

There are greater Cs to hold in thoughts in communication, regardless of the fact that they have got constantly been omitted:

The creativity - the speech can be greater amusing at the same time as you use sentence shape creatively. It is innovative whilst you operate seek phrases creatively.

Credibility - this indicates you ought to create a honest surroundings in a communique. A shiny and outstanding tone can gain it. It specifies the statistics you are speakme and includes accurate records.

Aspects of Effective Speaking Skills

Effective speaking way saying a few trouble you want, being heard, and the message is acted upon. There are some additives of speaking competencies. They encompass: the terms to use, the voice, tonal model, and nonverbal communique.

The phrases to apply depend masses. The listeners will come decrease back to the word you said and take a look at what you supposed and what to remember.

The intention marketplace - the terms you pick out out will range at the listeners. For instance, the phrases you operate on children will range from the terms you pick out to talk together together with your colleagues. The terms you operate on 3 hundred people in a conference will range from the ones you operate to speak with, as an example, board members.

Short sentences - they may be clean to recognize and but can create earnestness.

Use a lot less complicated language. If you can not supply an explanation for the terms you used, you did now not get the message.

The voice can monitor hundreds approximately a person's emotional kingdom. A man or woman's voice can supply a lack of shallowness. This approach that someone with low arrogance speaks in a low voice, while a person with self belief speaks in a commanding voice, resulting in readability of the message. It is critical to come to be acquainted with and command the sound of your voice. It is possible to report your voice and thoroughly pay attention to it. Most people dislike the sound of their very very own voices due to the reality they are embarrassing.

The more you switch out to be familiar with the sound of your very very very own voice, the less difficult it's going to in all likelihood be to keep a proper communication. By recording and paying attention to the sound, you becomes more acquainted in conjunction with your voice, resulting in a good deal less difficult communique.

Vocal Production

Anyone who wishes to turn out to be an active speaker need to very own those elements:

- Clarity – to be understood

- Volume - to be heard

- Variety - along with hobby

Clarity: When humans talk with their teeth in a decent function, and first-class have slight movement on their jaws, they turn out to be inaudible. To articulate nicely, you want to loosen up the jaw, exposing the mouth, and deliver whole advantages to all sounds that you make. Consequently, this could help your listeners examine your lips.

It is the rate of speakme, too. When you communicate too fast, the addressees will now not have the time to confirm what you're announcing. It's usually an outstanding indication to vary velocity at the identical time as speaking. Sometimes you have to quicken and then lessen, and it'll assist keep hobby.

Volume: Sometimes, you need to growth the quantity of your voice, and unique instances, you have to lower the quantity to create the emphasis. When you lessen your amount to a whisper in a sentence, you'll make the goal market rapid alert. Always be cautious no longer to abuse the technique, because it will lose the effect.

Inflection - Stress. When speaking to a crowd, try to bring the records with as good enough vocal power and zeal as feasible. This doesn't propose that your speech should be unrestrained. Try to make the speech as amusing as feasible. Emphasize a few phrases and expressions whilst speakme to carry significance.

Pause: Having a damage in court docket docket times is dominant in a speech. They can be used to highpoint the effectiveness of the proceeding announcement or advantage thoughtfulness in advance than the vital document. Dramatic breaks convey authority and self assurance in a speaker.

In any vital speech, it's usually beneficial to have a voice training. The voice is an essential tool for a speaker. The duration of heat-up will rely on how a good deal speaking you need to do.

Speaking to a Group of People, Always Take Note of These Signs

Blinking: When the target marketplace is staring and blinking fast, constantly apprehend the concern might be stupid or beneath deliberation.

Those who are avoiding eye touch: This can be an indication that the man or woman has low esteem.

Rubbing one eye: When a speaker rubs one eye regularly, the speaker has problems about the reaction from the goal marketplace.

Feet: When the target audience stamps their ft after a assertion, it method the goal marketplace modified into in agreement. And while the speaker stamps their toes, it usually shows a loss of sureness in what modified into said.

Fingers: When a speaker is rubbing a forefinger and a thumb together, they're retaining all over again a few component.

Smiles: Sincere smiles are normal, and most facial expressions are quick. If a smile is come what can also twisted, you're probable searching at a faux one.

How to Improve Communication Skills

Make conversation a right of manner: This approach that the message you're talking must be your priority. Read books and magazine articles to beautify your vocabulary.

Be sincere and stay at the message: This way you need to use single terms and easy language.

Engage your listeners: Let the communication be interesting with the beneficial aid of asking questions and inviting evaluations. This will draw the listeners to the conversation.

Take time to reply to a remark or a question: After listening, take time to apprehend and draft the response.

Make certain the audience can understand your message. Don't blame the listener for not understanding your message. You should make clear and rephrase the terms so that everyone can recognize the message.

Develop a listening potential: If you need to make bigger first rate verbal exchange abilties, learn how to listen first. Also, you want to now not be distracted by using manner of considering what you want to say or responding to a remark. Always reply; in no way react to a remark.

Watch out for your frame language: A extra massive part of communication is nonverbal; this shows usually seeking out for the seen signs from the listeners, like a shaking and nodding of the top. Also, be aware that your body is likewise sending signs and symptoms.

Maintaining eye touch: Whether you speak to a crowd or one person, generally keep eye touch. By doing this, you'll show which you care approximately your listeners and you're a credible individual.

Respect: Understanding the message isn't always about displaying that you in fact care about your listeners. Showing authentic contend with the desires of the target market will display recognize. The other manner to expose admire is via taking note of their responses.

Chapter 16: Developing Your Body Language

Even in case you don't enjoy confident, the use of confident frame language allow you to enjoy extra self-assured and better about your self ultimately. People who be bothered with the aid of social tension illness (SAD) often battle to hold their self-self notion while interacting with others. On the opportunity hand, you could boom yourself-self notion with the useful resource of making sure that your body language conveys a top notch message approximately yourself.

Develop your capability to undertaking an air of self-guarantee through way of operating towards the ones gestures and moves. The adage "faux it 'til you are making it" may be useful in a few conditions.

Make Direct Eye Contact

Maintaining eye touch in some unspecified time inside the destiny of social interactions let you seem extra confident. Good eye contact communicates to others that you are involved and comfortable in their organisation. Approximately 60% of the time, you ought to take a look at the opportunity man or woman. If making direct eye touch with a person feels too intimidating, begin via looking at a few aspect close to their eyes.

Lean Forward to Show Interest

When you are having a communication, leaning beforehand shows that you're paying interest and interested. As masses as it is able to be tempting to keep a sure amount of distance at the identical time as you're socially disturbing, doing so sends the message which you are fed up or unfriendly.

Maintain a Straight Posture

Don't be a slacker! Those who be by using social anxiety have a propensity to attempt to absorb as little location as possible, resulting in them sitting slumped over in a defensive function. Make a right now decrease returned, pull your shoulders some distance from your ears, and uncross your arms and legs to finish the pose. Taking up physical area permits you to venture a extra assured demeanor.

Maintain a Positive Attitude

When you are strolling, do you keep your eyes at the floor? When you're talking, does your head usually seem like bowed? Alternatively, walk with your head held immoderate, and your eyes focused beforehand. Although it can seem peculiar earlier than the whole lot, you may ultimately grow to be familiar with this more assured posture. Afterwards, you may use it while you're popularity and talking on the telephone (it will make eye contact a whole lot less hard, too).

Don't Fidget

Fidgeting is a commonplace symptom of hysteria and anxiety, and it ought to be taken significantly. Fidgeting need to be stored to a naked minimal to provide the impact of more self guarantee. Moving your knee or tapping your arms on a desk at the same time as speaking can detract interest from what you are pronouncing and make it tough for others to pay attention on what you are attempting to speak.

Keep Your Hands Out of Your Pockets

When you are worried approximately your arms shaking, shoving them into your wallet can be tempting. However, doing so makes you seem a lot much less confident and more demanding. Keep your palms from your wallet in case you need to seem more assured.

Reduce Movement Speed

Fast movements give the effect that you are extra anxious. Everything out of your hand gestures for your on foot stride ought to make a distinction; take some time and be aware the manner you enjoy more confident even as you're taking it slow to do topics slowly.

Take Longer Strides

Try to take longer strides to make amends for your slower pace at the identical time as you walk. The steps of people who are confident are big, and they bring approximately themselves with authority. You will experience lots much less worrying because of doing so.

Keep Your Hand Position in Check

Keep your palms far from your face and neck, as each are signs and symptoms that you are anxious, worried, or afraid, so exercising caution. These forms of movements aren't made with the useful resource of assured people in their skills. Making a steeple along side your fingers or retaining your fingers out can, but, communicate confidence.

Have a Firm Handshake

A shaky or limp handshake shows a lack of self-guarantee, so workout shaking fingers with self perception whenever you meet new humans. It becomes second nature after a few exercise.

Mimic the Body Language of Others

We frequently try this unconsciously. We sit up straighter while our companions reap this, or we gesture more frequently on the identical time as we're inside the enterprise of people who use their hands to speak. Incorporating a few different individual's frame language demonstrates that you are taking note of them, which let you benefit greater information and it'll make stronger your dating. In addition, if you have a robust bond with someone, you could experience extra snug and confident on your courting.